Abba's
PROMISE

33 Stories of God's Pledge to Provide

Abba's PROMISE

33 Stories of God's Pledge to Provide

DEBRA L. BUTTERFIELD

CROSSRIVER

BREWSTER, KANSAS USA

Contents

Why Thirty-three?

You might be wondering why thirty-three devotional stories are in this book. After all there are either thirty or thirty-one days in a month, not thirty-three.

I chose that number because in biblical numerology thirty-three means promise, and this book is all about God's promises.

To grasp the surety of His promises, we must understand a few things about His attributes.

He is perfect.

Think about that for a moment. Now consider a few more of His many attributes. He is omnipotent — no being possesses more power. (God can squash Satan like a bug any time He likes.) He is omniscient — no being knows more than He. He is omnipresent — present everywhere at every moment.

If some other being were more powerful or more knowledgeable or also omnipresent, wouldn't you be more inclined to worship that being rather than the God of the Bible? Wouldn't that also make God less than a god?

In his book *The Knowledge of the Holy*, AW Tozer states, "Any failure within the divine character would argue imperfection and, since God is perfect, it could not occur."

So now, let's consider the truth of James 1:17: God never changes. He is immutable — He never differs from himself.

Again quoting from Tozer's *Knowledge of the Holy*, "If He is unchanging, it follows that He could not be unfaithful, since that would require Him to change."

To fail to meet His promise is to be unfaithful. And He cannot be unfaithful. So as Hebrews 10:23 NLT says, we can "hold tightly without wavering to the hope we affirm, for God can be trusted to keep his promise" for "Every word of God proves true" (Proverbs 30:5 NLT).

It is my desire that the thirty-three stories of *Abba's Promise* will encourage you and grow your faith. Like Paul, "I pray that God, the source of hope, will fill you completely with joy and peace because you trust in Him. Then you will overflow with confident hope through the power of the Holy Spirit" (Romans 15:13 NLT).

—*Debra L. Butterfield*

Abba's Promise

for our

FINANCIAL NEEDS

"And if God cares so wonderfully for wildflowers that are here today and thrown into the fire tomorrow, he will certainly care for you." — Matthew 6:30 (NLT)

For Our Needs and Wants

Kelly F. Barr

"So do not worry saying, 'What shall we eat?' or 'What shall we drink?' or 'What shall we wear?' … But seek first his kingdom and his righteousness, and all these things will be given to you as well." — Matthew 6:31, 33 NIV

For many years, I struggled with trusting God for provision. If I couldn't see we had the finances to provide for our needs, I felt like I needed to do something to get the money. Usually, this resulted in thinking I needed to get a job, but my husband and I are the parents of three adopted sons. Our first son needed me to be home with him, so we made the decision I would be a stay-at-home mom.

My husband worked jobs that had a slow season. He would get laid off for some months of the year, usually near Thanksgiving or Christmas or just after, times when extra money was needed, though we never spent extravagantly even for Christmas. There were also times when my husband faced a permanent layoff because the company he worked for was either closing or downsizing. This sent me into a panic. How would we pay our bills, put food on the table, or provide for our basic needs?

But my husband never panicked. He trusted God to provide, and God did. Even if it was nothing beyond our basic needs, our needs were always met. We've gone many years without things wanted and without vacations, but have always had our needs supplied.

In addition to being a stay-at-home mom, I also became a homeschool mom. I made friends with women whose families had also chosen to live on a single income so they could raise and teach their children the values they felt were important.

I began to see God shower us with even more blessings...

These ladies taught me how to make more foods from scratch, even bread, which helped us save money. I already shopped at a discount grocery and only went to a regular grocery store for items the discount grocery didn't carry. I also became a frequent shopper at our local dollar store. I was learning to trust, but also did what I could to minimize the financial need — being a good steward.

My husband has always been faithful in paying tithe. He believes being faithful in giving back to God is a large part of why God is faithful in providing for us, just as He had instructed Joseph to provide for the seven years of famine in Egypt because Joseph was faithful to God even in the hardest times of his life.

As we faithfully tithed and I learned to trust God for His provision through the years, I began to see God shower us with even more blessings by sometimes providing some of the things we wanted, in addition to our needs. For example, one year we wanted to get our, then two, boys bicycles for Christmas but didn't have the money. God provided by someone giving us an anonymous monetary gift with a note that even suggested we use it to purchase bicycles for the boys for Christmas!

The most amazing thing God provided for us came near the end of October 2010. I received a phone call from the private agency we worked with to foster-to-adopt our children. A local building company had contacted them and asked them to choose a family to have work done on their home who wouldn't be able to afford to do it on their own. They chose us! We could choose one project to have done to our house, something like having the kitchen remodeled, or new flooring put in, or finishing our basement to create more living space.

After talking it over with my husband, we decided to ask to have the basement finished, as that was something we had been wanting for quite some time. The building company came out to look things over and said it would be fairly easy to create both a family room and an additional bedroom down there.

However, the project grew. Other companies kept donating for this annual "Day of Caring" project, providing funds above the original project budget. The woman who became my contact person with the building company, called me frequently, and came out to the house one or two more times to take measurements for additional work.

In the end, they created a family room and bedroom in our basement, and fully furnished them for us. They remodeled my entire kitchen and our little half-bathroom, provided all new carpet and flooring for most of the house, painted two complete floors of the house, and replaced our patio door, which had been in bad shape. They also provided all new appliances!

Since receiving that huge blessing, I no longer doubt God's hand of provision. When we face financial difficulties, I simply pray and wait, then I sit back and watch God work and praise Him for His goodness and blessings.

When you are faced with challenges in your life, remember God is there. Remain faithful in prayer, then wait, and you will see God's hand of provision in His timing.

Fishes and Loaves

Tracy Crump

*"There is a lad here, which hath five barley loaves,
and two small fishes: but what are they
among so many?"* — *John 6:9 KJV*

My son Jeremy tapped a gavel on the table. "I call this meeting to order."

The roomful of 4-H'ers quieted as the children, well-versed in the proper conduct of a business meeting, prepared to give their various committee reports.

After the minutes and treasurer's report, I asked to take the floor. "I'm sure most of you know Kenny and Kelly Johnson in the Explorers 4-H Club. I just found out that their dad, James, suffered a major heart attack a few days ago and had emergency surgery. Worse still, doctors found another problem that will require a second operation."

In as simple terms as possible, I explained the abdominal aortic aneurysm physicians discovered during James Johnson's bypass. As a former nurse, I knew an aneurysm left untreated was like a ticking time bomb. Eventually it will rupture and cost the patient his life.

"The doctors said Mr. Johnson will have to recover from his first surgery before they can operate for the aneurysm. But there's one more problem." I hesitated. "The Johnsons don't have any insurance. He was within three days of being eligible for insurance benefits at his new job when he had the heart attack. I know they would appreciate our prayers."

As soon as I sat down, ten-year-old Aaron rose. "I move that we do a fundraiser for the Johnsons."

I feigned a smile. A sweet thought, but the Johnsons needed money now. Besides, I didn't have time for that kind of monumental undertaking. I looked around the room and could tell other mothers were thinking the same thing, but... I looked again. The children's eyes were shining.

Finally we agreed to pray about it, and I was assigned to ask the Johnsons for permission to conduct a benefit in their name if we elected to do it.

At the next meeting, I sensed excitement in the air.

"Mr. Johnson is improving from his first surgery," I said. "His wife said they would appreciate anything we could do to help them. Because of their insurance status, the hospital requires a $500 deposit. The surgeon insists on payment for the first surgery before he will consider a surgery date to repair the aneurysm. The cardiologist is asking for money, too, and they simply don't have it."

"Then we'd better get moving. Why don't we rent a booth at May Fair and sell baked goods?"

"How about a spaghetti supper?"

"Why not both?"

And these were the mothers talking.

Things happened so quickly, I could hardly keep up. Four

moms put their lives on hold as they raced to help a family in distress. The phone lines burned between our homes. May Fair organizers told us it would cost $100 to rent a craft fair booth and then gave us the booth at no charge because "it's for a benefit." The town paper agreed to advertise the fundraisers at no cost.

One mom took it upon herself to cart her brood of five around to different businesses in our small town asking for donations of merchandise to raffle. Within two hours she had ten items, ice to chill the bottled water we planned to sell, and an offer from a printing company to print raffle and spaghetti supper tickets plus make signs for our baked goods booth — all free of charge. My head was spinning after she called to tell me of her bonanza. By that point, it was evident God's hand was on the project.

By the end of the day we had made $600...

Donations of baked goods poured in on the day of May Fair. One couple cooked homemade sausage and biscuits, arranged them in a pretty basket, and walked around to the other booths selling them. An out-of-town vendor heard of the benefit and donated one of her crafts to add to the raffle items. By the end of the day, we had made over $600. On baked goods and $1 raffle tickets!

The spaghetti supper proved even more incredible. A teen 4-H'er contributed 200 home-cooked rolls that rivaled those from a popular restaurant chain. A friend, whose husband worked for a food distributor, donated spaghetti sauce complete with meat, salad dressing, and even butter. People baked cakes and pies to sell at the dinner. That only left us paper products, pasta, and bagged salad to purchase, and we were all set.

The dinner went off without a hitch. After dishing our last plate of spaghetti that evening, we tallied up the number of meal tickets redeemed and calculated we had made around $400, maybe $500 total with the additional raffle tickets sold. But after counting the money, we found we had almost $1100! Everyone was flabbergasted. Just like the fishes and loaves, God had multiplied our feeble efforts to provide for someone in need.

Altogether, the James Johnson Benefit accumulated over $2100 — not a grand sum, perhaps, and certainly not enough to pay for open heart surgery, but it was more than we ever dreamed of making. We sent a $500 deposit to the hospital and split the balance between the two doctors, wondering where the Johnsons would get the rest of the money for surgery.

When the cardiac surgeon heard about the benefit, however, he told Mrs. Johnson, "If you have that kind of backing from the community, I'm not worried about getting my fee."

Mr. Johnson had successful aneurysm surgery and recovered quickly to return home to his family. Just as importantly, a group of children and their moms learned a lesson about trusting in God's provision.

God knows what we need even before we do. Although He could "rain pennies from heaven," He often uses other people to answer our prayers for provision. Have you ever received an unexpected bonus or monetary gift when your account was drained and bills were due? Has someone shown up at your door with a bag of groceries when your shelves had just gone empty? We can trust God to provide.

Snapshots of God's Provision

Nancy Kay Grace

"And my God will meet all your needs according to the riches of his glory in Christ Jesus." — Phil. 4:19 NIV

The first year of our marriage in 1975 brought adjustments as we learned to trust God for our finances. Rick had just graduated with his bachelor's degree and I had one more year of college to complete my degree. Our long-term plan was for him to attend seminary to become a full time pastor. Rick had a part-time weekend youth ministry to supplement a full time sales job. I held a part-time position at the university bookstore with about eight hours per week. Neither of us had extravagant spending habits, but we still had to make adaptations in spending our limited resources. The financial advice we received in our pre-marital counseling was "Give ten percent, save ten percent, and spend the rest with joy and gladness."

We had to depend on God as we learned to stretch our meager finances to pay rent, utilities, food, and tithes. We prayed that our needs would be covered. When the income didn't match the outflow, we cut back in the areas of food and entertainment.

One particular day I felt discouraged while praying about our financial needs. When I went to the mailbox, I found a plain white envelope addressed to us with no return address. Curious, I turned it over and slid my finger under the flap. Inside was a hand-printed note that read, "Thought you might need this." Unfolding the piece of paper, I found a $20 bill inside. Tears of gratitude stung my eyes. The Lord had heard our prayers, provided a blessing, and encouraged my heart.

I felt humbled that God provided for us in spite of my grumbling.

This was the first of several snapshots of provision where the Lord showed us His trustworthiness for our daily needs.

Every Saturday and Sunday, we traveled fifty miles to work at a church in youth ministry. The agreement was that the church provided housing and meals for us while we were there and pay a small amount each week. Though the compensation wasn't much, we thought this would be valuable to give us early ministry experience.

Our weekend adventures in ministry began. As the months passed, we noticed that the church wasn't fulfilling the promise for our meals. One Sunday night we were weary and hungry after the youth group meeting. We had to fill the car with gas and wouldn't have much money left for groceries for the week. The long, dark ride home would seem even longer with our stomachs growling.

After a short discussion, we decided to stop at a drive-in restaurant to get a basket meal to share. We knew we didn't have a lot of money for fast food and purchasing this meal was an extra expense. The carhop brought our basket meal of chicken strips and french fries to the car. Written on the bill was "This one's on me. I've wanted to have you over for a meal. Enjoy!" We looked inside the restaurant where a church member smiled and waved to us. I felt humbled that God provided for us in spite of my grumbling.

Months later, we thought about buying a home instead of renting an apartment. At that time a house payment would be the same as rent. We found a small home and proceeded to apply for a loan. Sitting on the living room floor of our apartment, we counted stacks of coins from our change jar to add to the loan application. We knew there was little chance to get approved, but thought it was worth a try. The loan officer was honest in telling us the loan probably wouldn't go through. Although we anticipated that, we still prayed for it to happen.

A few days later the loan officer called. "Kids, I am surprised. The loan is approved." We were astonished! We trusted in our heavenly Father who would supply our needs. We could have a home as a place to share God's love through hospitality.

Recalling these snapshots of God's provision in the mail, a chicken basket meal, and a coin jar reminds me of looking at faded photographs from decades ago. On recognizing the pictures, I clearly see how God used those challenging times to develop deeper faith and trust in Him. These instances had a profound effect on me as I learned to trust God with our finances early in our married life. I saw His faithfulness each time, and with each episode, my trust grew.

Though the scenes have faded, the truth of God's faithfulness to provide has remained vibrant. Those long ago lessons laid the foundation of trusting God. They bring warmth and hope to my heart even now, as we have celebrated our fortieth anniversary. God's hand has provided all our needs through the years of raising our family with active kids, braces, and college expenses. He will continue to provide as we anticipate retirement.

No need is too small to bring to God. His promise in Philippians 4:19 is sure: "And my God will meet all your needs according to his glorious riches in Christ Jesus."

Small Potatoes

Merrie Hansen

*"These hard times are small potatoes compared
to the coming good times, the lavish celebration
prepared for us. There's far more here than
meets the eye." — 2 Corinthians 4:17-18 MSG*

Potato patties again?" My sweaty twelve-year-old son tossed his baseball mitt on the kitchen counter next to the long yellow and blue box.

"Yep." I poured two whipped eggs into the cold mashed potatoes left over from the night before and gave a raised-eyebrow look at his glove. As I mixed the ingredients, he put away his mitt, washed his hands, and then pulled a sheet of waxed paper from the box. Together, we formed the white mixture into patties.

As a self-employed, homeschooling, financially challenged family, we prayed for God to provide in whatever way He deemed suitable… and this was an especially financially challenging time.

Calls for computer service came less frequently for my husband, so he took a part-time summer job at the co-op elevators during wheat harvest to supplement our shrinking income. I did as much creative bookkeeping as I could to keep the lights lit. As a family, we revived lessons from our grandparents in stretching our food budget. We took turns washing and drying dishes when the dishwasher went on the fritz.

The boys learned about coupons and store specials. Their math skills improved as they calculated weights and prices for best buys (not always the store specials or the use of coupons). They picked up aluminum cans from the ditches and redeemed them at the recycling center to have a little spending money in their pockets. Their dad used the opportunity to teach them the art of changing the oil and other simple money-saving tricks for maintaining our cars. And the most important lessons were patience in trusting and waiting for the Lord to provide as He did for the people we studied from the Bible every day in school.

Abraham, Isaac, and a ram: "Then Abraham looked up and saw a ram caught by its horns in a thicket. So he took the ram and sacrificed it as a burnt offering in place of his son. Abraham named the place Yahweh-Yireh (which means 'the LORD will provide'). To this day, people still use that name as a proverb: 'On the mountain of the LORD it will be provided.'" Genesis 22:13-14 (NLT)

Moses, the Hebrew children, and the sea: "But Moses told the people, 'Don't be afraid. Just stand still and watch the LORD rescue you today. The Egyptians you see today will never be seen again. The LORD Himself will fight for you. Just stay calm." Exodus 14:13-14 (NLT)

Elisha, a widow, and some oil: "'Then go into your house with your sons and shut the door behind you. Pour olive oil from your flask into the jars, setting each one aside when it is filled.' So she did as she was told. Her sons kept bringing jars to her, and she filled one after another. Soon every container was full to the brim! 'Bring me another jar,' she said to one of her sons. 'There aren't any more!' he told her. And then the olive oil stopped flowing. When she told the man of God what had happened, he said to her, 'Now sell the olive oil and pay your debts, and you and your sons can live on what is left over.'" 2 Kings 4:4-7 (NLT)

Paul, God, and secret of contentment: "I have learned how to be content with whatever I have. I know how to live on almost nothing or with everything. I have learned the secret of living in every situation, whether it is with a full stomach or empty, with plenty or little.... this same God who takes care of me will supply all your needs from His glorious riches, which have been given to us in Christ Jesus." Philippians 4:11, 12, 19 NLT

So, the day I came across a fifty-pound bag of potatoes at a great price, I shed a tear as I looked at my sons. "The Lord has provided again." My twelve-year-old vegetable-hating son scrunched his face at me, but nodded with understanding. His older, less vegetable-hating brother grinned and groaned as he loaded the heavy find into our grocery cart.

Each time I see a big bag of potatoes, I hear the groans of my then teenaged sons and delight in the faith I see in them as adult men today. Those hard times in our house were small potatoes compared to the joy of teaching our children God's faithfulness through His promise to provide for all of our needs.

Landslides

Londa Hayden

*"Then Abraham looked up and saw a ram caught
by its horns in a thicket.… Abraham named
the place Yahweh-Yireh (which means 'the Lord
will provide')."— Genesis 22:13, 14 NLT*

Anxiety engulfed me as I watched our home gutted and the cost to rebuild skyrocketed. Black mold had penetrated the walls and brought with it a landslide of hardships.

Living in an apartment for ten months with three active boys was no easy task either. That's six feet stomping up and down stairs and running across our upstairs apartment floor. Despite all my efforts to keep them quiet, our downstairs neighbors were not exactly thrilled.

What can I say? Boys will be boys. Kids will be kids. My special needs child having meltdowns on top of all that, didn't help either. This particular complex was not so kid friendly or understanding. Consequently, the management disapproved, which forced us to move again.

Several other families attending our church in Houston, Texas, suffered through similar ordeals. There were concerns shared about how insurance companies may no longer pay for rebuilds, which compounded my fears. We prayed, and shared

Scripture and laughter through these troubled times, but then a series of unfortunate events hit our family.

Our middle son suffered through an adverse reaction to an antibiotic, which left him bed ridden for weeks. Thankfully, no lasting health issues arose on his full recovery. Immediately following this incident, the family dog bit our youngest child in the face, requiring our son to have emergency surgery. Our beloved golden retriever of fourteen years had to go into quarantine. My husband and I then made the difficult decision to put down our dear companion for fear he may bite again, or bite another child other than our own. Shortly

Our son broke his elbow while in-line skating, resulting in — you guessed it — another emergency surgery.

thereafter, our other son broke his elbow while in-line skating, resulting in — you guessed it — another emergency surgery.

I managed to keep my sense of humor by telling everyone we were now on a first name basis with the medical staff at the local hospital emergency room. To be honest though, I felt all my prayers were hitting the ceiling and that God must be ignoring me. What was going on?

Our church family kept praying for God's provision, but doubt gripped me. When the day came for the insurance adjuster to determine the payout for our rebuild, I dreaded what he may not do for us. I bit my lip awaiting the verdict. Would he determine an adequate amount to cover all the expenses involved to replace everything we'd lost? To my amazement, we received a substantial amount. How could I have been such a doubting Thomas?

Finally, the day came for us to move back home. The entire house was like new and I had the kitchen of my dreams, but soon the winds of change began to blow again. My husband's job transferred him. With much sadness, I prepared to move our family to a new state, completely uprooted and not knowing a soul.

My husband managed to fly home every other weekend, but this left me with the daunting task of caring for the house, the kids, the bills, everything for four months. Securing a brand new house was on the horizon, but we had to sell our current house first. Just days after listing, the invasion of Iraq threatened nuclear war on America. The market stopped cold as the world held its breath.

The Realtor assured me things would pick up soon, but day after day passed with no potential buyers in sight. To make matters worse, the corporate buyout was denied because of the previous mold infestation. Even though God's provision had come through for the rebuild, my doubts and fears started once again. Maybe I didn't deserve any more than what God had already given me. Can we really ask too much from our Jehovah-Jireh?

Again, our church group prayed with us and we waited and waited and waited. I asked God to bring a buyer for our house and to renew the company's faith in honoring the corporate buyout. Sometimes the best learning experiences happen during these waiting periods.

Another month passed ever so slowly. It was all I could do to breathe, the anxiety and pressure to sell our home so intense. Finally, the market opened up again and like an unblocked river, the potential buyers streamed through our house. Two weeks before the movers were scheduled to arrive, we got an offer for our asking price. A renewed corporate buy-out offer for more than the asking price came on the same day. God didn't just answer one of my prayers. He answered both my requests with a resounding yes, which left me amazed at His overwhelming love and graciousness.

Since then, I've suffered through even worse situations. When doubt starts to come — and it does — I'm always able to point back to this very significant time when Jehovah-Jireh came through for me with flying colors. Proverbs 3:5-6 tell us, "Trust in the LORD with all your heart and lean not on your own understanding; in all your ways submit to him, and he will make your paths straight" (NIV). He may not have answered me when I wanted Him to, but He did answer in His time, which is always incredibly perfect no matter how late it may seem to us.

A landslide of blessings followed a landslide of hardships, and through it I was reassured of Jehovah-Jireh's faithfulness to provide for His own. I learned to trust God and that nothing was too big for Him to handle. Just as He provided for me today, and for Abraham thousands of years ago, He'll provide for you.

Unexpected Source of Provision

Mason K. Brown

"And my God will meet all your needs according to the riches of his glory in Christ Jesus." — Philippians 4:19 (NIV)

We decided not to purchase the house of our dreams — a Spanish-style home on a large corner lot, with fabulous schools in one of the nicest neighborhoods in the county. Our children were unhappy about our decision — they would miss the in-ground swimming pool. Their father and I disliked the property's drainage problems that caused the deep end of the pool, when filled with water, to float clear out of the ground in the winter and spring.

In addition, there were numerous other issues with the home itself that had not been disclosed to us when we signed our lease with an option to buy agreement. We were not going to exercise our purchase option. We would spend the remaining year of our lease looking for an affordable, acceptable home in the neighborhood.

During our housing search my husband hurt his back at work. His employer, the State of California, disputed his injury claim. For months he received no salary. My smaller salary was enough to either make our lease payments or everything else, not both. We struggled to keep up, but in spite of our best efforts and fervent prayers we fell further and further behind.

We felt like we had been cheated and lied to about the house we were living in, but believed God had a purpose in all things. We had agreed to a certain monthly lease fee and knew we were responsible for paying that amount. We were trying. Not only were we not keeping up with our current obligations we were unable to save any money toward the purchase of another home.

When the doorbell rang, I hesitated to answer it. I assumed it would be more bad news. When I went to the door and saw the landlady standing on the porch I wished I had followed my instinct to run and hide. I knew she had come to demand money I wouldn't have for a few more days.

"I know you don't want to see me," she said, "but please let me talk with you. My husband and I are getting a divorce. He was not honest with you about this house. There are many things wrong with it and you probably don't want to buy it. In good conscience, I cannot sell it to you. I'm letting the bank repossess it. I don't want you to pay me any more money. You can live here free until the bank tells you to move out. That will probably be a year or more. However long it is, you are welcome to stay."

I could hardly believe such generosity. She had every right to continue collecting our rent.

Earlier in the week I had called our state legislator and told him my husband's plight with his salary and work injury claim. Shortly after the landlady left, I received a phone call from the representative's office. They had resolved the issue of my husband's claim and he would immediately be awarded back pay for the time he had been off work, and he would begin receiving regular compensation and benefits according to the state's payroll schedule.

We spent twelve more months in our house. The children enjoyed another summer with their swimming pool. A bank representative did come by a few times and offered us a very good deal. But we had calculated the cost of repairing the drainage and the other issues, and decided it wouldn't be worth the price. Besides, it seemed obvious to us God did not want us to stay there when He had so clearly provided a way out.

I could hardly believe such generosity.

We used my husband's back pay to catch up bills we had fallen behind on, and saved the money we would have spent making lease payments. When we found the home we were looking for, we had a sizable down payment saved. The house was just one block west and one block south from the old location — an easy walk for the kids to visit their friends. We were able to stay in the same great neighborhood with the wonderful schools. The new house had an above ground pool — not quite as good in our children's opinions — and no drainage problem — a huge improvement from our point of view.

I always remember the plaque my grandparents had hanging in their home when I was a child. It has been hanging in my home now for many years. "And we know that in all things God works for the good of those who love him, who have been called according to his purpose." Romans 8:28 (NIV) Even in this time of deep struggle and stress, God turned what often felt to me like a hopeless situation into a time of great blessing and joy.

While I worried about my family being homeless and hungry, God softened the heart of a non-believer, providing for my family in ways I never would have imagined. God, in His wisdom, foresaw all the nightmares accompanying the home of our dreams. Sometimes, when weighed down with all the struggles of a difficult situation like the one we found ourselves in, I forget that God has everything under control. He sure picked an awesome way to remind me.

The Late Check Provided

Diane Nunley

"Therefore I say to you, do not worry about your life,
what you will eat or what you will drink; nor about
your body, what you will put on." Matthew 6:25 NKJV

At a time when I was in between jobs, I turned to crafting to supplement my income. The small checks I received helped provide for my needs, but I never imagined a check that didn't come would not only provide, but also convince me of God's perfect timing and steadfastness.

The anticipated payment at the end of the week from a regular customer had to be delayed when her husband's illness required her to accompany him to an out of town hospital. Fridays usually found my purse empty. Her situation was totally understandable but threw me into a near state of despair. My pantry held enough peanut butter until I resumed regular employment, but my ailing dog needed her prescription food to treat a severe gastrointestinal ailment.

"Just thirty dollars, Lord," I prayed as I drove to the post office to pick up the afternoon mail.

Like so many people, I had the idea that it was my situation and my efforts that provided: a good job, generous family, or having someone to share my expenses. The panic I felt at not being able to provide for my ailing animal stemmed from this erroneous belief.

The post consisted of the usual junk mail, bills, and notices. But a small, handwritten envelope with an unfamiliar return name and address caught my attention. The letter explained that the enclosed check was for goods purchased at a craft show six months previous. The customer had misplaced my address.

I still had a half hour to get to the bank and cash the check for $33 and change. I made it to the vet before closing, purchased my dog's special food, and came home in time for her regular feeding and my dinner of a peanut butter sandwich.

A small, handwritten envelope with an unfamiliar return name and address caught my attention.

That evening as I meditated on this experience, I realized the Lord always knows what I need, and He provides exactly for these needs in His perfect timing. I had read many times of the faithful provision for George Mueller's orphans, mystified at each account of the miraculous timing of the knock on his door resulting in milk and groceries. Yet, I had to admit I believed

I was out of God's hearing when it was me who called. Orphans and a great missionary were important; I was a plain person with a sick dog.

Paul explains in Philippians 4:19 that "my God shall supply all your need according to His riches in glory by Christ Jesus" (NKJV). He refers to our spiritual need being fulfilled by the presence of Christ in our hearts. Yet, many scholars also attribute this endless capacity to provide to include needs of this world. Matthew tells us much the same thing. "Therefore I say to you, do not worry about your life, what you will eat or what you will drink; nor about your body, what you will put on." (Matthew 6:25 NKJV)

After this experience, I made a commitment to tithe as an obedient act to God who provides, and experienced confidence that the Lord truly is in control as I rest in Him. I continued to work but I ceased striving. I could be still and know that He is God. (see Psalm 46:10 NKJV)

Each of us can review our experiences with need and provision to conclude that a God who directs the seasons and provides for every sparrow has unlimited resources. He desires for us to depend on Him and not on ourselves. Nor does He want us to seek worldly solutions to our problems when He is always ready to intervene on our behalf. His methods may not seem clear to us at the time, but in retrospect the path will be seen as the route to His outstretched arms where we are safe, loved, and cared for.

Now when I find myself in need, I know to pray for wisdom. I seek to understand if I am being trained to wait and know Him more deeply. I may not have because He knows I don't need it now, or it may be that the blessing is reserved for a special moment in my future when my need will be the greatest.

Like the prophet Habakkuk, "Though the fig tree shall not blossom, nor fruit be on the vines; Though the labor of the olive may fail, And the fields yield no food;… Yet I will rejoice in the LORD, I will joy in the God of my salvation." (Hab. 3:17, 18 NKJV)

I am now retired and satisfied not to have a job. My journey has provided me with a testimony of the Lord's provision through many years of dependence on Him. He has never failed even when I fell into temptation to doubt. When the tempter whispers, I shout back that a check that didn't come proved to me God's Word is truth and He is ever faithful.

Trust the God who frequently says "I will" in His Word. Pray to Him to reveal His depth of provision within your life. Make your requests known to Him and receive His peace. Rejoice and be joyful in your need. He is our Jehovah Jireh, the God who provides.

One Thousand Times Blessed

Teri Lyn

"But my God shall supply all your need according to his riches in glory by Christ Jesus." — Philippians 4:19 KJV

For nearly three years I lived in South Korea as an instructor teaching English. One autumn, as I boarded the plane to return to the United States for a visit, I was unaware I had failed to file a certain form with the consulate, and on my return to South Korea, the authorities confiscated my visa. Re-issuing a work visa required a trip out of the country. This news devastated me since I had returned with little money and needed to go back to work immediately.

My frozen bank account held 3,815 won, equivalent to $4 at that time. Due to me was 2,000,000 won ($2000) for a writing project I had completed months earlier. The publishing company could not remit the funds due to my visa status.

The closest country to South Korea is Japan. Three weeks after my return to South Korea, my employer handed me round-trip bus and ferry tickets to Japan and a paid hotel reservation for one night. I packed some snacks and would be gone thirty hours at most. If I needed money, I could go to an ATM and get a few dollars through my US credit card, but if not, then those won and US dollars in my wallet would carry me through.

A huge problem occurred immediately on checking in at the ferry office. Required taxes and fees had to be paid in Japanese yen before boarding the ferry, and my credit card would not work at the ATM.

"Hey, Lord, please show me my next step," I pleaded, knowing He was my only hope. I was directed to the monetary exchange booth, and by combining won, dollars, and some loose coins, I paid the taxes. I left the exchange counter and boarded a hovercraft that airily transported more than 300 people three hours from Buson, South Korea, to Fukuyama, Japan.

"Father, thank you for blessing me. But what am I to do with no money for taxes upon my return?"

"I will take care of all your needs through my riches in glory in Christ Jesus," I heard. Those comforting words calmed my concerns, and I realized just how often He had intervened for me over the years. Pulling out a good book, I read occasionally and gazed through partially opened windows at the clear skies and gentle waves forming beneath the craft.

Upon debarking, I saw a young English speaker, also in Japan to reinstate his visa, who boarded the bus with me and then pointed me to my bus stop motel. The motel clerk told me the way to the consulate the next morning. The consulate was efficient, and I returned to the ferry terminal by 1:00 only to learn that the hovercraft was canceled due to forecast storms. Finding a way to change my ticket and pay the taxes concerned me.

In the downstairs corner room of the huge ferry office building, no English-speaker existed, but after much confusion, a young man finally called another who understood my needs.

He hurriedly exchanged my ticket and handed me some cash, a refund for overpayment. Cost of the hovercraft was higher than the transport ferry that could carry passengers safely through rough seas. The refund was just enough to pay the taxes.

I boarded the ferry and was led to my cabin shared by ten others. We found our places on the spotless floor next to cabinets holding blankets and pillows provided for each passenger. The stormy, eight-hour trip back to Korea was ferocious. Comfort arrived from a lovely couple. The gentleman spoke English and told me of his experiences in the S.K. military where he earned rank as a colonel. His lovely wife, Su bin, could not speak English. But that didn't matter; we exchanged womanly talk through our hands and her husband's interpretation.

What am I going to do with no money for taxes upon my return?

About halfway through the trip, the colonel left and returned with three heavenly cups of coffee. I pulled snacks from my pack, and Su bin did the same. We shared a meal Korean style, with all the food placed before us and partaken in shared contentment. Su bin had freshly cut fruit among other delicacies; I had pre-packaged health bars — which she swiftly cut into pieces — and some vegetable chips. They bowed to pray before Su Bin passed out chopsticks. Our conversation covered their faith in Jesus Christ and dedication to a Nazarene church, and I was able to share my love for our Lord with them.

Once the ferry arrived in Buson, I found we landed in a different port from the one in which I had departed. Su bin, from across the room, noticed my disconcerted and tired face, and she insisted we share a taxi to the bus terminal. They paid the fare and remained with me until my bus arrived. The colonel walked me to my seat and gave me a bottle of water. I was penniless but for the taxi fare tucked tightly inside my bag that would take me from the bus terminal to my apartment in Gwangju.

Less than two weeks later, my employer received my South Korean government paperwork. He had me sign the proper forms, and I was able to call the publisher to receive pay. One day later, I walked to the bank. I expected 2,000,000 won, but found 3,185,000 won ($3,185) — exactly 1000 times the bank balance of the past five weeks. My employer had deposited the remainder. He said before departing for the States months earlier, I had worked but not yet been paid for those hours.

When the Lord chose to bless me after a long trial, I could only praise Him. He provided beyond measure, and He let me know He truly does take care of all my needs. We humans falter when times get tough, but we need to remember that He cares immeasurably.

God's Promise

of

HIS PRESENCE

"Even when I walk through the darkest valley, I will not be afraid, for you are close beside me. Your rod and your staff protect and comfort me." —Psalm 23:4 NLT

Promise of His Presence

Melody Balthaser

"He fills my life with good things. My youth is renewed like the eagle's!" — Psalm 103:5 NLT

During my mother's bout with cancer, we were able to keep her in the comfort of her own home and under the care of my aunt and myself. It was an excruciatingly painful journey for my mother as her mind and body deteriorated.

Caregiving took its toll on me, and when my mother passed away, I found myself emotionally raw and physically depleted. Worse than that, I felt spiritually confused. Did I ever really know God? How could a God who is love allow His children like my mother (and my brother before her) to suffer such agony?

Over the next ten years, I was determined to understand God, or at least to better understand His ways and to find some sort of peace. I knew healing, in its purest form, could only come from Him. After all, He created me and knew my deepest secrets, struggles, and longings. If He didn't know what I needed, then no one did.

I found a church and a mentor who kept me uncomfortable and digging deeper into the Word, which in turn revealed more of my own issues. I pleaded with God to speak to me and reveal His heart. I learned He speaks in many ways beyond what I was taught as a child, and I was on high alert for His voice.

Hopping into my friend's car in wintry weather, we would travel all night to get to conferences. We were hungry for God and full of anticipation and expectancy of what He would do.

At one of these conferences, a woman told me she had a vision of me in a sauna. As I sat in the steam, which was the fragrance of the Lord's presence, I got younger and younger! She quoted Psalm 103:5 to me and then said, "The Lord will renew your youth like the eagle's as you rest and bask in His Presence. Resting in Him will be invigorating and revitalizing."

I learned He speaks in many ways beyond what I was taught as a child.

This word encouraged me. I went home with determination to stop striving and start resting and trusting that my healing was at hand. I needed to embrace the fact that Jesus had made a way for me. I didn't need to work for anything. It was already available to me and I simply needed to be quiet and open to receive.

At that point in time, I had never seen an eagle in the wild. Since then, I see eagles everywhere. They fly over my car as I drive down the road. They swoop over my canoe as I paddle down the river. On windy winter afternoons, I watch a pair of eagles that catch air currents and circle higher and higher into the sky above my house.

One day, I was helping my husband in his sign shop and our young son came running in the door.

"Mommy, your eagles are sitting in the tree!"

We went outside to witness a pair of eagles perched at the peak of the tree above our shop. They peered down at us for several minutes before flying off.

During an early morning drive to the grocery store, I pulled over to observe a huge bald eagle as he sat atop a dead tree by the side of the road.

Especially stirring was when my daughter and I were in Zambia riding through an animal reserve. Among zebras, giraffes, and monkeys, we spotted an African eagle in a tree over our jeep.

Whenever I see an eagle it brings a smile to my face because I know God is confirming His Word to me. It is a gentle reminder of His promise to me and an invitation to spend time with Him.

Our Father is always communicating with us and He confirms His Word in a variety of ways. If we are too busy running here and there, we can grow weary and wonder where He is. He calls out to us to be still so we can see, hear, and feel His love for us. His promises are yes and amen (2 Corinthians 1:20). They are eternal.

As Psalm 103:5 says, God satisfies our desires with good things and renews our youth like the eagle's. We need to slow down and rest in Him in order to be revitalized and invigorated by His presence. Then we become aware of His loving communication to us and He will give us all we need. Out of this place of rest comes great accomplishment. Not of our own making but out of His presence.

Allow the Father to come into your chaos and confusion. Rest in His presence and trust Him to satisfy and renew you.

His Guiding Presence

Catherine Ulrich Brakefield

*"Our Father in heaven, Hallowed be Your name.
Your kingdom come. Your will be done On earth
as it is in heaven." — Matthew 6: 9–10 NKJV*

I grew up the oldest of six. My father was of German descent and my mother Scotch-Irish. Needless to say, living with my parents was never dull. Mom felt it her duty to keep Dad on the narrow pathway and "Our Father in heaven," became their favorite Bible verse, especially the "Your kingdom come, Your will be done" part.

Knowing God's promises included another kingdom to explore and that His guidance was unfailing, encouraged my parents' faith to believe dreams can come true. It was just the natural thing for me to follow their lead.

Whenever I wanted to quit, Dad told me, "You can do anything you want to do if you put your mind to it." Dad heard those same words from his father, while growing up in Detroit. They were good enough for him to grow up on, so they were good enough for me.

When I expressed my ten cent allowance wasn't sufficient, my dad's favorite argument was that during the Great Depression he peddled papers before school in Detroit and gave all his earnings to his father.

But that wasn't the end of the argument. Dad got out a paper and pencil, and asked me to tell him everything he and Mom provided for me in the way of food, clothing, and education for the past year.

Well, I could see where this was heading, so instead, I decided to forgo any more discussion regarding an allowance.

Growing up during the Great Depression taught Dad and Mom the value of a dollar. Fighting the Germans in Italy during WWII taught Dad the value of life and that prayer was the channel to Jesus.

Whenever I started to complain about my weekdays and weekends being taken up with church, I got an earful of what children today might think a lecture. For me, it was a living history lesson about life.

As my dad's words fell on my head with fervor, I pictured him elbowing his way through the mine fields, the machine-gun fire blasting in his ears, bullets dimpling the dirt in front and behind him as dust and debris flew into his mouth and eyes.

Dad said this was the time in his life he learned how to pray, and I wasn't too young to learn that Christ can only lead you if you're willing to follow. "Learn that," Dad said, "and you'll be too busy praying to be scared when life deals you a stacked deck."

When I asked him about his buddies getting killed all around him, he'd tell me it was just their time and that "You'll never find an atheist in a fox hole."

The greatest test to God's guidance in my life came in an unexpected way.

Dad had just come in from work. He slammed down his briefcase and asked, "Where's your Mother?"

"In the kitchen," I said and promptly followed.

When parents mumble, that's a dead giveaway something major is about to happen, and that's when my ears are their keenest.

"Margaret, I'm quitting my job. My boss is moving the plant to Port Huron. I'm going to start my own engineering company, right here." Mom and Dad descended the stairs of our Cape Cod home to the lower level of the spacious room that had its own entrance. My siblings and I loved playing here.

"See, I can buy some drafting boards and set them up here, what do you think?" Dad's eyes looked hopefully to Mom. I knew then Dad wasn't going to quit his job or follow his dream if Mom said no.

Mom was nine months pregnant. She rubbed her extended belly and said with a tear glistening on her cheek, "Ok, Nibs, you know what you're doing."

I knew then Dad wasn't going to quit his job or follow his dream if Mom said no.

Lean years followed, the odds of successfully starting a fabrication plant were astronomical. Another stacked deck. All the collateral they had was God's guidance and protection.

"Thy will be done, Jesus," I often heard Mom say. Little jobs that paid the bills trickled in. Encouraged, Dad and Mom moved forward. What began in the bottom floor of our Cape Cod home became the second largest privately owned con-

51

veyor company in Michigan.

"No one thought I could do it," Dad told me when I was grown. "But God kept opening doors, so Margaret and I stepped through them."

Always the life of the party, Dad and Mom could waltz with the best of them. Mom was always quick to give her leading partner the credit. She helped me see my role in my marriage — to be a partner and not the leader.

That's when my life tests began. I learned marriage was a commitment between God, husband, and wife. I realized it wasn't through my parents' words, but through their example that I witnessed God's guiding presence and promise fulfillment. I learned the art of patience, remembering my parents' trials. I understood the answer to my prayers might not come immediately. God will test my faith.

My dreams took years of toil and commitment before I witnessed that prayer-seed strong and beautifully formed into a tree of blessings that impacted my life. My parents' example and God's guidance led me through the debris of despair with faith, hope, and love. Because only God's infinite love bears all things, believes all things... endures... and endures and accepts that "His will be done."

Mom died January 6, 2006, and Dad died six years later to the day. I can still hear his words: "Christ can only lead you if you're willing to follow. Learn that, and you'll be too busy praying to be scared when life deals you a stacked deck."

God promised His guidance through the pitfalls of life, His protection in our darkest hours, and eternal life in His kingdom to come for those who believe. He provides what He promised.

May our prayer be "Let Your will be done all the years of my life" as we trust in His guiding presence.

Faith and a Steel Pipe

Marilyn Wilhoit Burell

"And Jesus said unto them, Because of your unbelief: for verily I say unto you, If ye have faith as a grain of mustard seed, ye shall say unto this mountain, Remove hence to yonder place; and it shall remove; and nothing shall be impossible unto you." — Matthew 17:20 KJV

God has unique methods of teaching us what it means to have faith. We are never too old or too wise for His lessons.

During the time my husband and I served as directors of single-adult work at our church, we learned more from our students than we ever taught. God provided surprising and great lessons in faith. Most of the time I was too preoccupied with my own pursuits to recognize them or learn from His teaching hand, but I was due for a lesson in faith wrapped in a steel pipe.

Houston holds its Special Olympics in one of our many stadiums, and the event always draws a large crowd, not only of parents and volunteers, but also of professional athletes and celebrities. Our single-adult group was large enough to sponsor a full event. Under the direction of the Special Olympics Committee, we were responsible for organizing, setting up, and executing our event. That year our event was the fifty-yard dash.

My assignment was to run in my own lane alongside the athletes for their protection as well as to shout words of encouragement. When the child crossed the finish line, it was my job to give him or her a big congratulatory hug and present the victory medal.

I met my athlete, a tiny girl about ten years old, who was totally blind.

After running several heats of children with a variety of disabilities, we were about to experience a special heat requiring meticulous staging. First, a cable was stretched from the beginning to the end of the outside lane — my lane! A steel pipe was placed on the cable as two professional athletes pulled the cable tight. I watched while another person swept the lane clean. There could be no obstacles for this special child, not even a small pebble.

I met my athlete, a tiny girl about ten years old, who was totally blind. My sympathetic tears were in sharp contrast to her bright attitude; she was not here for sympathy, but to win! I placed her little hand on the pipe and told her to hold on tight and to run as hard as she could when she heard the starting gun. I promised I would be with her all the way and her reward would be waiting for her when she crossed the finish line. She had to trust me and run as fast as she could.

With the blast from the starting gun, that little girl who

could see nothing, bolted and ran with a fierce determination, holding onto the pipe and trusting me. I ran alongside her shouting, "Keep running, honey, you can do it. ... Sweetheart, just keep running! I'm here! Just keep running!" When she crossed the finish line with cheers from the crowd, I swept her into my arms for a big bear hug and draped the victory medal around her neck. She won. She had finished the race!

I see great similarities between the faith of my tiny blind athlete and Christian faith. We are so blind, but when we put our hands in His, we simply have to run because He holds on to us and has promised to never let go. "And I give unto them eternal life; and they shall never perish, neither shall any *man* pluck them out of my hand. My Father, which gave *them* me, is greater than all; and no *man* is able to pluck *them* out of my Father's hand." (John 10:28-29 KJV)

In Hebrews we hear the challenge of the starting gun, "Wherefore seeing we also are compassed about with so great a cloud of witnesses, let us lay aside every weight, and the sin which doth so easily beset *us*, and let us run with patience the race that is set before us." (Hebrews 12:1 KJV)

The race set before us may at times seem dark and harsh, but if we listen with our heart instead of our head, we can hear Him gently say, "Keep running, you can do it, just keep trusting. I will be with you all the way, I will make a path for you through the obstacles, and I will protect you and encourage you. Your reward is waiting for you when you cross the finish line."

Our Christian walk can exhibit the same kind of strong faith as my little blind athlete. With our hands in God's, He can help us to run flat out by faith. He will pick us up when we stumble, give us a vision when we are unable to see, and hold us close when we stray from Him. I pray that at the end we each will be able to say, "I have fought a good fight, I have finished *my* course, I have kept the faith." (2 Timothy 4:7 KJV)

I raise my hands in honor of the God who is always with me.

Surrounded by Love

Debra L. Butterfield

"I have loved you, my people, with an everlasting love. With unfailing love I have drawn you to myself." — Jeremiah 31:3 NLT

When I saw the job opening listed in the newspaper for an administrative assistant at Focus on the Family, I couldn't apply fast enough. I failed to get the job, but the human resources assistant suggested I join their temporary administrative assistant pool — I'd fill positions around the ministry while departments searched for full-time employees. If no one was temporarily in need of an admin assistant, I'd have no work — and no income. As the sole earner for my family, no income presented big problems.

I'd been working in another temp job for nearly a year. That company offered me the position full time because they didn't want to see me leave. What did God want me to do? Take a secure, but unfulfilling job or take a risk on a job that might or might not fulfill my dream of being a writer? I wrote down the pros and cons of each. The temporary position at Focus on the

Family came out on the bottom — way down on the bottom. I prayed fervently for God's guidance, but my life was in such disarray, I couldn't hear His voice.

Four years earlier my husband had been arrested and later tried and convicted of sexually abusing my twelve-year-old daughter (his step-daughter). I'd spent the last four years working to bring my children and myself through the fallout. My daughter was in and out of foster care; my oldest son was in trouble with the law and in correctional custody. Knowing I had to care for my three-year-old son was often the only thing that kept me going.

If I was ever going to make a better life for my children and me, and make some of my dreams a reality, now was the time.

I took the temporary position at Focus knowing full well in a few months I could find myself unemployed. They placed me in the position I had directly applied for but failed to get. I'd been a stay-at-home mom for ten years, so I couldn't blame anyone for not wanting to take a chance on me. Now God had provided another opportunity to get that same job in their in-house advertising department.

I had been working there about three weeks when they offered the position full time. I agreed. From the git-go the people in the department treated me like family. They were glad to have me and appreciated my skills. On Secretary Appreciation Day, they decorated my desk chair like a throne and gave me a dozen salmon-colored roses. I wasn't used to being treated that way — by employers or family.

Rejection was a common occurrence in my childhood, and the added hurt and betrayal from two husbands compounded the problem. I had drawn so far into a protective shell only God's love could draw me out.

Our daily routine started with departmental devotions. In this safe atmosphere I got better acquainted with my coworkers and witnessed their own vulnerability about the struggles and needs in their lives. Their treatment of me as an equal began to draw me out.

I don't remember at what point I told them about what my husband had done and the battle I faced every day in finding healing for my daughter, my other kids, and me. This confession could have pushed them away. Instead, they kept showering me with their love. The more they accepted me for who I was — trials and all — the more it drew me out of my shell.

My boss saw a potential in me I couldn't see. When another position in the department came open a year and a half later, she offered it to me. I was flabbergasted. Her belief in me sent a hammer crashing into what remained of my shell. I served in that position for about two years before applying for a junior copywriter position in the same department.

Almost four years to the day of accepting a temporary job, I stepped into a copywriter job and my dream of becoming a writer began to see sunlight.

My time there was my gateway to the Promised Land, but

from the world's viewpoint a tremendous gamble. What I learned there has served me well and often in my life as a freelance writer and editor, but I would never have had the confidence to step into my dream if I hadn't been loved out of my shell. God knew the people there would be channels of His love.

The true miracle of my seven years working for Focus on the Family isn't that God fulfilled my dream as a writer, but that He used my time there to bring what I needed most: healing to my shattered soul and spirit. Life had delivered unspeakable wounds, but the people of Peak Creative department loved me as brothers and sisters in Christ are called to love.

God commanded the Israelites to erect memorials as a physical reminder of His deliverance and provision in their lives. We need to do the same because when we are in the midst of crisis it's all too easy to forget what God has done for us in the past. When we look at our difficulties, we are tempted to doubt God. But when we look back on all the times He answered His promises in our lives — even those needs we didn't see for ourselves — our doubts drop to the wayside.

"Let us hold tightly without wavering to the hope we affirm, for God can be trusted to keep his promise." (Hebrews 10:23 NLT)

Courage

Laure Covert

"The high and lofty one who lives in eternity, the Holy One, says this: 'I live in the high and holy place with those whose spirits are contrite and humble. I restore the crushed spirit of the humble and revive the courage of those with repentant hearts.'" — Isaiah 57:15 NLT

*I*f I am honest with myself, I know I'm a coward by nature. When I look back on my life, now that I am a woman who is over the hill, I see many times when I've been afraid and didn't try something because of cowardice.

But on closer examination, I also see other episodes when I received just enough courage — the special kind only the Lord can give — to step onto new ground. I went to Christian college far away from home; I traveled to foreign countries on missions trips; I ministered to refugees in inner city Chicago; I moved to Colorado so my husband could pursue his counseling degree; and I homeschooled my three kids — the first in my family to do so.

I believe God gives the gift of boldness, a synonym for courage, to empower us to accomplish those purposes He knows only we can fulfill. The apostles experienced boldness as a direct result of the filling of the Holy Spirit as recorded in Acts 4:31 (NLT): After this prayer, the meeting place shook, and they were all filled with the Holy Spirit. Then they preached the word of God with boldness.

Even though courage to speak the truth of the gospel is one of the most vital, God wants to fill us with courage for other actions: making a move to a new home or city, applying for a new job, adopting a child, etc. However, even seemingly insignificant moments of bravery matter.

Recently I was asked to accompany my church youth group to Mexico as a Spanish interpreter and a mother figure. As we prepared to go, the youth pastor told us all we needed to set our hearts to respond with a yes to whatever ministry activity we were asked to do. That seemed easy for much of the trip because I found comforting homesick teen girls and cheering on my fellow team members to be fairly safe and familiar activities.

Then God threw me a curve ball.

One day, after I finished explaining, in Spanish, the meaning of our drama presentation to a group of local Mexican children, the missionary and local pastor approached me and asked me to come to their church the next day to preach a thirty-minute sermon in Spanish. Although I obediently answered in the affirmative, I was terrified — I had not preached from the pulpit before and never in Spanish.

As I rode back to the hotel in our van full of chatting, laughing students, I stared silently out of the grubby window with a mind full of "Oh Lord, help!" thoughts. We wound through narrow streets with brightly painted adobe walls on either side almost close enough to scrape the paint off the van. The walls served as the equivalent to our billboards, advertising local businesses. As I stared numbly out the window, incoherently praying for courage, I saw this ad in vivid blue painted on the wall "Más de 35 años de experiencia" (More than 35 years of experience).

The Lord gave me a personalized message to stir up my courage and confirm His call to do that frightening task because He knew I would recognize the number 35, which represented the years I have known Him personally. That was the requirement for this task, not my preaching credentials or experience.

The next morning, with insides quivering, I took the microphone, placed my open Bible and scribbled notes on the podium of the church sanctuary, and offered a stirring thirty-minute message — all in Spanish — to my Mexican brothers and sisters.

Then God threw me a curve ball.

The process by which our heavenly Father stirs up courage in us varies case by case, episode by episode, but the truth remains — He provides the boldness.

We may wish, in vain, to know what is around the next bend. The urge to play it safe in the familiar routine of our present lives often trumps our willingness to offer ourselves without reservation to God for His purposes. The best way to live, albeit scary, is also the only way to please Him. Like Isaiah the prophet, we look up trustfully at "the high and lofty one who lives in eternity, the Holy One" to receive the courage we need to do what He asks of us.

What task do you sense the Lord asking you to step out of your comfort zone to complete? Perhaps it is something new or maybe it is a call He gave you in the past that He is reviving. He has promised to provide and He is faithful. Now is the time to ask Him for a fresh dose of courage.

An Everyday Miracle

Theresa Jenner Garrido

"For he breaks down gates of bronze and cuts through bars of iron." — Psalm 107:16 NIV

When my sister's family left Seattle to relocate in Georgia, I followed, but it was a tough transition. We missed the mountains and trees from home. It wasn't long before my sister and brother-in-law made a momentous decision: find property in the foothills of the Smoky Mountains. The sooner the better.

Aware their limited resources wouldn't go far, they spent hours researching properties until they found their little piece of heaven-on-earth. Fifteen wooded acres in the North Georgia Mountains at a price they could afford. The perfect outlet for six sons and one daughter; the perfect panacea for my hard-working sister and brother-in-law and for me, a middle school teacher, drowning in lesson plans.

A few weeks after purchasing this dream property, our elderly father, still living in Seattle, announced his plan to visit. The day after he arrived, we filled the car-top carrier with sleeping bags, tents, and supplies; squeezed kids, adults, and one dog into the SUV and, in high spirits, left Atlanta for a three-day camping trip. We couldn't wait to show Dad our mountains since he still held the conviction that no place on earth could compare to his beautiful Washington State.

Anticipation swelled as we made the slow, tedious drive up the narrow, winding roads. Tuning out the rambunctious kids in the back, my sister and I focused on Dad, whose face now registered dawning appreciation. As we neared our destination, he fidgeted in his seat like his grandchildren and cheered the loudest when we finally reached the gate. Our property bordered the easement set aside for power lines owned and managed by Georgia Power and shared a narrow gravel road.

No one expected the gate to our road to be closed or locked.

No one expected the gate to our road to be closed or locked. Dad voiced his bewilderment and the kids moaned when my brother-in-law, after studying the situation, shook his head and lifted hands in resignation. The last time he and my sister visited the property, the gate had been wide open. The possibility of a closed and locked gate never entered his mind.

One by one we piled out of the car. The older boys fiddled with the padlock while Dad and my brother-in-law tramped through the underbrush on either side of the barricade. My sister and I stayed by the car and fought frustrated tears. Our plans dissipated like so much smoke in the wind. No camp fires or marshmallow-toasting tonight. Dad would not experience the beauty we'd discovered in our new state, never know that, even though far from our beloved Pacific Northwest, Georgia still laid claim to a bit of God's Country.

An awful silence consumed the minutes as we each digested this disappointment. Finally, my brother-in-law sighed and told everyone to get back in the car. Nothing to do but head for home. It would be dusk soon and he didn't want to drive the unfamiliar mountain roads after dark.

Hearts heavy, we steered the kids back to the car but paused when we heard something. As one, we turned to see a battered sedan appear from around the bend and roll to a stop. An elderly man, dressed in baggy cords and an old mackinaw, clambered out, while his companion, a woman with a cap of gray curls, remained in the passenger seat, smiling and fluttering fingers in a gentle wave.

The stranger walked up to my brother-in-law and shared half a dozen words. Before we knew what was happening, he thrust a gnarled hand deep into a coat pocket and came out with a set of keys. Nodding at my sister and me, he approached the gate and with two flicks of his wrist, unlocked it and kicked it open. Offering one last nod but without saying another word, he returned to his car and climbed in. After managing a tight turn, he nosed the car back the way they'd come. In minutes his car disappeared and the forest settled into silence.

For several heartbeats we remained frozen in a tableau of incredulity. Then in tandem, we adults joined the kids in the car. My brother-in-law started the engine and drove through the yawning gate. No one, not even the five-year-old, uttered a word.

Needless to say, we had our glorious three days in the mountains. Dad hiked the property with his grandsons and son-in-law and relished everything he saw. The sun shone brightly during the day, and a million stars filled the sky at night. We even toasted marshmallows.

No one forgot the magic of what happened that fateful evening. My brother-in-law, determined to unearth the identity of our rescuer, asked around and even confronted Georgia Power about the mystery man — a man, who chanced to drive up a mountain road in the middle of nowhere at sunset, had a key that fit the lock of a gate we needed opened, and disappeared as quickly as he materialized — but nobody could offer an explanation. To this day, we are convinced the old man was an angel.

Over and over, God demonstrates His desire to provide for us. There have been other gates in my life that needed unlocking yet received no heavenly assistance, and day-to-day struggles with locked doors overwhelm me at times, but I only have to recall that one special gate to immediately feel better. Miracles still happen today.

We really do have a Father who will break through barriers to please us. Even barriers we think impenetrable. We have a God who delights in doing the impossible. We just have to ask and trust and accept.

"Believe me when I say that I am in the Father and the Father is in me; or at least believe on the evidence of the works themselves." (John 14:11 NIV)

T.R.U.S.T.

Barbara Gordon

*"Even youths shall faint and be weary, and young men
shall fall exhausted; but they who wait for the* Lord
*shall renew their strength; they shall mount up with
wings like eagles; they shall run and not be weary; they
shall walk and not faint." Isaiah 40:30-31 ESV*

My heart plummeted when I received the news
my daughter-in-law had failed the state board
test. Sadness welled up inside and I blinked
back tears. Disappointment washed over me and anger threatened to surface. How could this be? Feelings of assurance that
God would provide were replaced with seeds of doubt.

I suppose not passing a test is minor compared to many
of life's disappointments, but it didn't feel insignificant to us.
No one is immune; setbacks are sure to come. How should a
Christian react in the face of seeming defeat? What does the
Bible instruct us to do when worry jeopardizes our peace?
How can we be sure He is the God who provides?

Proverbs 3:5-6 provides the answer: "Trust in the Lord with
all your heart and lean not on your own understanding; in all
your ways submit to him, and he will make your paths straight"
(NIV). Trust Him — two small words — but packed with wisdom. How does one trust the Lord in the face of disappointment?

69

This acronym provides practical steps to put trust into action.

> **T** - *Talk to God*
> **R** - *Read God's Word*
> **U** - *Utilize wise counsel*
> **S** - *Sing praises*
> **T** - *Time*

I talked to God about my disappointment; I told Him my heart hurt for Angie. I reminded Him — as if He might have forgotten — that I had prayed she would pass the first time, and asked others to pray the same.

In the quietness of my time with the Lord, He reminded me I've also prayed my children would draw close to Him. He told me it's usually through trials we grow to be like Christ. I have to admit I reacted like a teenager, rolled my eyes, and said, "Whatever." Nevertheless, talking to God was the first step toward healing and the realization He does provide.

Reading God's Word also reminded me of His never-ending provision. Jonah was disappointed when God didn't destroy the people of Nineveh. Mary and Martha were disappointed when Jesus didn't show up in time to heal their brother, Lazarus. Imagine the disappointment of the disciples when Jesus was crucified. As we examine these accounts, we know the end of each story and realize things weren't as they seemed. God had a plan, one not immediately obvious. In our disappointments, we, like the heroes of the Bible, learn to trust the One who always provides.

Utilizing wise counsel in our times of anguish helps us overcome our natural negative reactions. The wisest man who ever lived penned, "The way of fools seems right to them, but the wise listen to advice." (Proverbs 12:15 NIV) While my tendency is to bear frustrations alone, I find that when I share my struggles with trusted friends, I gain a right perspective. God's provision often comes in the form of wise counselors.

Acts 16 relates the account of Paul and Silas in prison. Unjustly thrown in jail, their feet in stocks, and hurting from the beatings they received, they sang praises instead of whining. Their praise resulted in the prison doors miraculously opening and the jailer and his family placing their trust in God. Again, God provided. While my disappointment was nothing by comparison, praising God brought relief as I focused on His greatness and not my weakness.

I have to admit I reacted like a teenager, rolled my eyes, and said, "Whatever."

The last letter in the trust acronym stands for time. Even when we pray, read the Bible, talk to others, and praise, it usually takes time to fully recuperate from loss. It's been several weeks since we received the upsetting results of Angie's score, and while the pain is still there, it's dimmed. While she studies with renewed vigor, I pray with restored hope. As we practice trusting, we learn to declare with the psalmist, "The LORD is my strength and my shield; my heart trusts in him, and he helps me. My heart leaps for joy, and with my song I praise him." (Psalm 28:7 NIV)

In light of the stress we face each day, it is no wonder we are susceptible to worry and defeat. Thankfully, God has promised to provide strength as we wait on Him. He is the God Who provides.

The Power of Praying Friends

Jean McLachlan Hess

"I have told you these things, so that in me you may have peace. In this world you will have trouble. But take heart! I have overcome the world." — John 16:33 NIV

It happened three weeks after my mother passed. I was home alone. The thought of a warm, relaxing bath flowed through my mind. Ten minutes, perhaps even twenty, soaking under some frothy bubbles would soothe my heart and calm my mind. The idea transformed into the perfect plan, and I set the plan in motion.

Bubbles sparkled in the light, causing glorious rainbows to dance around as I stepped into the bath. Luxury, sheer luxury, I thought, as I burrowed under the warm blanket of foam. Exactly what I needed. Time to remember and reflect. The days had rushed by after my mother's death; finally I was able to think without noise and distractions. Peace, beautiful peace.

I knew I couldn't linger too long in this state of luxury. The family would be home soon. I began the preparation to leave my indulgent oasis. Just one more minute, and then I'd force myself to step

73

out of this tranquil state. Sitting up, I gave myself a quick wash.

A lump! I wasn't looking for one, but I found one.

The tranquility of the moment dissipated as quickly as the bubbles were bursting around me. My body now demanded my full attention. My peace took flight and in its place came fear. I wanted only rest and peace, and now that peace had disappeared.

Dear Lord, I found a lump. What should I do? Who should I tell? Perhaps fear made me decide not to tell my children. Perhaps, if I didn't talk about it out loud, it might not be true.

I knew I needed God's help, but somehow I was too paralyzed to ask. In the end I called two friends.

I found a lump. I wasn't looking for one, but I found one.

They both promised to pray for me. It was Saturday evening and I assured my confidants I would seek an appointment with a specialist on Monday. Fear consumed my thoughts and sleep evaded me. Daylight was a welcome friend.

On Monday morning I got up and prepared for the day. I'm not sure how much time passed before I noticed something. Something wonderful. Something miraculous. My fear had gone and peace filled my heart. What happened to my fear? My circumstances had not changed, but my heart, mind, soul, and spirit had.

God heard the prayers of my dear friends. He saw me, His daughter, struggling, and He sent me His peace. What a glorious gift! Now I could face whatever lay ahead. Instead of crippling fear accompanying me as I made my way to face the upcoming tests, peace — a deep, powerful, and much needed peace — was my companion.

Eventually, I received good news from the doctors. The lump was nothing more than a cyst that needed drained.

Jesus warned us, "In this world you will have trouble." Thankfully, He had more to say. "But take heart! I have overcome the world." He established His peace in the midst of my storm. He promises to establish peace in the midst of your storms, too.

If you are currently in the midst of a storm, Jesus is right there with you. He desires to comfort you and to strengthen you. He will wipe your tears and hold you close to His heart. His presence will fill you with His peace.

Let the Holy Spirit remind you of the words of Philippians 4:6-7, "Do not be anxious about anything, but in every situation, by prayer and petition, with thanksgiving, present your requests to God. And the peace of God, which transcends all understanding, will guard your hearts and your minds in Christ Jesus" (NIV).

I Will Carry You

Sandra L. Hickman

"Even to your old age, I am He, And even to gray hairs I will carry you! I have made, and I will bear; Even I will carry, and will deliver you." — Isaiah 46:4 NKJV

In 2006, at age 52, I journeyed to South Africa and then to Zambia for seven life-changing weeks as a missionary. Like being thrown into the deep end of the pool, trepidation and excitement coursed through me.

Was I really doing this? I had desired to be a missionary to Africa since I was a child. I wanted God's perfect will, so I asked Him to confirm this journey. I needed His stamp on it, assuring my safety. I sought His protection promised in Isaiah 46:4. "I will carry you" lingered in my heart.

After a prayer meeting, a visiting Indian pastor approached me. "Ma'am, I have a word for you from the Lord. He says to tell you that He is watching over you. The devil tried to kill you many years ago and you were supposed to die, but the Lord says it was I who protected you!"

I could scarcely believe my ears.

"I'm not sure what happened to you, but I believe it was an accident." He continued, "But God says I will look after you. This scripture is for you, Isaiah 46:4 'Even to *your* old age, I *am* He, and even to gray hairs I will carry *you*! I have made, and I will bear; Even I will carry, and will deliver *you*.'"

"Do you understand what God is saying?" the visiting pastor asked.

With stunned realization that God was speaking, I answered, "Yes. Years ago, I was in a terrifying car crash with my two small daughters. I hit a semi-trailer truck. The front of my car was ripped off and flung through the air. We went flying down a ditch in an accident that police stated should have killed us all. They couldn't believe we survived, completely unscathed."

The Indian pastor and I stared at each other. We knew this message was truly from God.

"Well," he said, "I don't know why the Lord is telling me this, but He wants you to know that He will look after you. It has been Him all along watching over you, even until you are old with gray hairs."

"I've been asking God for confirmation of a mission trip to Africa... if I would be safe!" Tearfully, I continued, "My prayer is now answered!" I knew God would carry me.

Before the trip, my granddaughters came for an overnight stay. Three beautiful baby girls ages one to three. The next morning I awoke with a headache. Driving them home to their farm, the pain in my head increased, gripping me like a skull cap.

I was driving on a lonely country road, bearing dreadful pain. Suddenly, through my driver's side window, I saw a black silhouette of a creature — grotesque, with a long body, long dangling arms, and long pointed wings. The word gangling immediately came to mind. It just hovered there, and I knew it was demonic.

Then to my utter amazement, a huge shadow of massive

wings spread over the car. I whispered, "Lord, what is that?" Was it an eagle's wings? But they were so huge! As quickly as those wings appeared, the gangling demon disappeared — instantly gone, along with my headache.

It all happened so fast, but my mind searched for answers. The children!

I glanced at them, knowing that demon was on assignment to kill me and my grandchildren. I began warfare prayer, covering us in the blood of Jesus, praying all the way to the farm, still awestruck at what happened.

Later, traveling home, as soon as I asked the Lord what those wings were over the car, He showed me a vision. It was an angel whose massive wings spread across my car. I cried and said, "Of course, Lord! Of course! It was an angel!" God proved when His angels come devils flee. His incontestable protection in action. God's promise is His provision.

The Indian pastor and I stared at each other. We knew this message was truly from God.

And God was faithful as He carried me safely throughout Africa. While in Cape Town, a dear sister in Christ brought me another confirming word from the Lord in Joshua 1:9, "Have I not commanded you? Be strong and of good courage; do not be afraid, nor be dismayed, for the LORD your God *is* with you wherever you go" (NKJV).

Have no fear. Know that God will provide for you. His protection is sovereign and nothing can contest it. Pray every day, until your spirit conquers your fearful flesh. Let nothing sidetrack you or prevent you from accessing His great promise of provision.

Healing of the Heart

Veronica A. Ryan

"The LORD is close to the brokenhearted; he rescues those whose spirits are crushed." — Psalm 34:18 (NLT)

I spent most of my young life watching friends and siblings catch the eye of someone, date, break up, and within a few weeks start dating someone else. I felt out of sorts, like I had forgotten something critical that could solve the mystery of my dating drought. As the years passed, I became more anxious. When would I finally be able to entrust my heart to a man? A good looking, faith-filled man with a great sense of humor.

In college, I met Michael. He seemed to have everything on my imaginary checklist for a future husband. We often sat in the musty yellow hallways of my college dormitory until the late hours of the night. As he peeled back little pieces of his heart, I marveled at his life's journey. When illness left me bedridden for two weeks, Michael stopped by often to keep me company and to regale me with more stories, movies, food, and loads of laughs. He sacrificed time from finals and other friends to be with me. From then on my admiration for him was cemented.

Finally, in the spring, I offered him my heart. With a smile on his lips, he listened to me declare my affection for him. Then he got up and left for a meeting. The topic was never approached by him again. Two days later, he employed a mutual friend to deliver the news. Instead of hearing the words I desired, I listened to the most painful rejection of my life. The memories of our late night conversations lost their sweet fragrance. I felt like a fool. I gave my heart to someone who examined it, set it down, and walked away.

As I knelt before the Lord in the chapel, stunned and hurt, tears poured down my cheeks. Where did I go wrong? I must have misread things somehow. Why didn't he say something sooner? Maybe he didn't know how to tell me. How could I have been so naïve to think he wanted to be with me?

No matter how many questions I posed to myself or God, one stinging truth echoed inside: I couldn't make Michael want me. As I simmered in my tears, another bitter thought slid through my mind and lodged itself in my throat. What if no one ever wanted me? What if I just wasn't enough? My soul wept at the harsh possibility.

I felt like a fool. I gave my heart to someone who examined it, set it down, and walked away.

Life was a mess after Michael's rejection. My roommate and I were not on good terms and most of my friends were unaware of the wound I carried inside. Soon after, Michael began to date another girl on campus. Each time I saw them a thorn dug deeper into my wound. I used to enjoy normal social encounters with men, now they only thickened the protective fortress I built around my heart. If God wanted a man in my life, then God was going to have to bring a sledgehammer.

I spent most of my free time in the chapel. There Jesus spoke to me in Scripture and gently began to heal me with His words. The more I prayed the more I trusted He would fulfill my desire for companionship in His time, not mine. I promised to no longer attempt to give my heart away. Instead, I gave it to Him. This small act freed me from my burden of anxiety. If a man wanted me, he would have to go to God, and this time I was willing to wait.

Walking into my history class one afternoon I plopped down in the first seat I could find. My head turned as a handsome man lowered into the chair next to me. One look at his gray-blue eyes and my heart stumbled over itself. Then I heard God whisper somewhere deep inside, "This is the one you have waited for." The fortress within me quaked at his presence yet welcomed the liberation. In a matter of years this man, with the help of God's heavenly sledgehammer, shattered my inner walls and claimed my heart for his own in marriage.

So often, we offer ourselves to the world in hopes of finding acceptance and love. When our offering is rejected, the natural reaction is to retreat deep inside a hardened fortress. Yet, God does not desire us to withdraw; instead, He desires that we entrust ourselves into His eternal care. One act of trust is all He needs. In His gentle embrace He will guide us to that which is true, good, and beautiful.

Give your heart where it can do the most good. Pray for guidance and follow the Lord's prompting. It may be something as simple as praying for your spouse every morning and with your spouse every night. Maybe God will ask you to put your phone away for an evening with your family. Whatever it is, big or small, trust that the Lord is with you and will provide you the grace needed to accomplish His will.

Through the smallest acts of trust, God can do great things and fulfill the longings of our hearts.

God Always Leads Us

Elisabeth Natter

"And the LORD went before them by day in a pillar of cloud to lead them along the way, and by night in a pillar of fire to give them light, that they might travel by day and by night. The pillar of cloud by day and the pillar of fire by night did not depart from before the people." — Exodus 13:21-22, ESV

I think I know how Abram must have felt when God told him to pick up and move. Not just himself, but all his tents, his servants, and his livestock. He began a life of wandering through the desert from place to place, going wherever God led, to the place that God showed him. He left the comfort, security, and familiarity of his home and headed into the unknown because he obeyed God's calling on his life.

I don't have flocks of sheep and goats and I'm not wandering vast lands in Asia, but I was once on the move following God's leading for a new direction in my life.

I began living with my mother two months after my father passed away. Immediately following his death, our family realized that my mother's dementia had progressed to the point it wasn't safe for her to live alone. But Mom's adamant refusal to move to a retirement community or even receive in-home assistance from complete strangers presented a dilemma. Following several months of deliberation, we finally settled on a plan that involved relocating my family to a larger home that would more suitably accommodate our family of seven plus one. Despite her protests, I would become Mom's live-in caregiver.

So began the upheaval. I quit my job and pulled our first grader out of school. I packed suitcases, homeschool books, computers, three kids, and the dog, and temporarily moved in with my mother to care for her until we could all comfortably live under one roof. My husband and oldest daughter remained in our home, one hour away, to begin house renovations while working and commuting to college. With schedules readjusted, we all tried to settle into the new normal.

But there was nothing close to normal about this scenario. My husband was trying to work and be a general contractor/do-it-yourselfer. The kids and I, with my mother in tow, made several trips back home for work weekends and attempted to assist in the renovations. But we never seemed to accomplish enough, and I always left feeling disheartened. We were torn apart again and not any closer to our goal of selling the house. It took five months before we added the finishing touches and placed the house on the market. There were times when I felt we would never finish, and we questioned if we should continue, but we always returned to believing God was leading us in this path.

Nine weeks later we had an offer and a request to settle in thirty days. We needed to move quickly. Fortunately, I'd become obsessed with an internet real estate site, Zillow, and had been searching for months for our ideal home. I'd viewed photos and read the descriptions of over 100 houses spread throughout three counties. The pros and cons of our top choices were laid out in a spreadsheet culminating in a final decision. After packing two medium-sized moving trucks and three cars, the move went forward. The season's first snowfall came on both our loading and moving days and we celebrated Christmas under a blanket of white in our new home.

But there was nothing close to normal about this scenario.

Ten months after this journey began, we were finally settled in our new home. God had brought us through periods of separation, strained moments in our marriage, times of doubting whether we were making the correct decisions, and hundreds of hours of physical labor to finally rest in a larger, more comfortable home surrounded by nature.

However, I really saw the true sign of God's provision present itself when after one week in our new home we realized we lived less than ten miles from a nuclear generating station. The facility has two cooling towers that continually release vast amounts of water vapor, filling the sky with a tall, white cloud column. On a clear day, the vapor can been seen over fifty miles away. In my travels, I could often see the cloud column rising high in the air and I always knew in which direction home lay.

One evening while standing at the kitchen sink, I paused to enjoy the evening sunset. Through the bare-armed winter trees the sky displayed a palette of red, pink, purple, and orange, and provided perfect back-lighting to the column of steam visible from our window. Illuminated by the glorious sunset, the cloud almost appeared to be on fire.

At that moment, I realized I was no longer on the move like Abram, waiting for the fulfillment of a promise. I was more like the Israelites being led out of Egypt. In this journey of caring for someone with dementia, God was moving before me, showing the way. He guided the Israelites with a pillar of cloud by day and a pillar of fire at night. God graciously provided me with a constant physical reminder that He is always with me, going before and guiding me in this long journey of caring for my mother.

We may not all have such dramatic physical signs of God's leading, but our heavenly Father reassures us of His constant leading. It may be through a sermon, a kind word of encouragement we receive, or a sense of unexpected peace we feel during a trial. God promises to never take His presence from us when we continue to follow His leading. Ask Him today to be aware of His leading and to trust in His continued care and guidance.

A Journey Through the Maze

Jill Printzenhoff

"Do not be afraid or discouraged, for the LORD will person-ally go ahead of you. He will be with you; he will neither fail you nor abandon you." — Deuteronomy 31:8 NLT

One fall Friday evening I took my oldest daughter and a friend of hers to a local flashlight maze. I had never been through a cornfield at night, so I wasn't sure what to expect. However, being one for adventure, and the fact that this had been on my to-do list for a while, I was really looking forward to roaming through the maze in the dark.

We entered the grounds of Cherry Crest Farms and were met with a festive atmosphere. For us, the mood changed to excitement as we stepped on to the maze path. Moving through the entrance of the maize, we approached a sign that gave us three path options: easy, intermediate, or advanced. Unanimously we decided to take the intermediate route.

We clicked on our flashlights and headed into the dark field in search of clues to guide us along our way. After a while we reached our first sign. The information on the back of the sign gave us directions to our next checkpoint, so we took off down the trail in search of our next clue.

Throughout our nighttime journey, we occasionally saw others who were on their own path, who at times, crossed over the same path we traveled. We were all looking for clues and puzzle pieces to fill in our maize maps. At one point in our adventure, my group happened upon a really long and dark path that must have been near the center of the cornfield. Until this point in our trek I had been quiet. When we turned down this path I uttered, "I'm glad I'm not out here alone. I think I'd be really freaked out by now." At that very moment, God reminded me of His presence, and how He has been with me throughout this journey called life.

I'm glad I'm not out here alone. I think I'd be really freaked out by now.

In reality, we are all on a journey with varying paths that cross in and out of the lives of others. Sometimes our paths are easy. Sometimes our paths are a little more challenging. And sometimes we find ourselves in the midst of an extremely difficult trek. I have personally been on some very rough roads that, had I known were coming, I would have been looking for an off ramp.

Going through a recent health crisis with our youngest daughter was one such road. However, this crisis led me personally to seek more of God through His Word and through prayer.

While I knew God was walking with our family through this event, there were times when I wondered if He was hearing my prayers for her healing, or if I was just talking to thin air. He seemed silent most of the time, which frustrated me. Often, through my frustration with this silence, I fervently verbalized my raw feelings. As a result, my anguished heart echoed some of the same words found in Scripture that Habakkuk and David both spoke long ago when they too were burdened. As strange as this might sound, it was comforting to know that others who have been through difficult journeys have also voiced their raw feelings to God and pleaded with Him in prayer for answers.

It took me several months to recognize that, although God seems silent, He does hear our prayers, He is listening, and He will rescue in His own way and His own timing. The key word is timing. My own selfishness wanted God to answer my prayers immediately, but God works methodically and on His timetable. It took more than ten months for my daughter's health to improve. During that time, God faithfully walked with us each day, and on days we were too tired to walk, He carried us through that journey.

I have no idea what road you are currently traveling. Maybe it's an easy road. Maybe it's an intermediate one. Or maybe it's a road of such difficulty you have no idea how you got there or if you will ever get through this particular journey. Rest assured, Jesus stands willing to walk with you, and to help guide you down each of life's roads. In fact, He's willing to carry you if that is what you need. Just keep trusting in Him and His promise to never abandon you.

Your Storm

Sharon Garlock Spiegel

"So do not fear, for I am with you; do not be dismayed, for I am your God. I will strengthen you and help you; I will uphold you with my righteous right hand." — Isaiah 41:10 (NIV)

Fear is the first and foremost emotion we experience when a storm is at its peak. I live in the part of the country where tornadoes present a real threat during the spring and summer. As a child I lived on the East Coast and remember the sights, sounds, and fury of going through a hurricane.

None of those dangers seem as devastating as going through the storms life brings our way. It's then that we wonder if God has forgotten us. The baby's sick, his fever raging — you've prayed until you can't pray anymore. Your teenager is out of control, nothing you do or say helps — you've prayed till you're hoarse. Your husband is in ICU and you don't know if he's going to make it. All your funds have gone to medical bills and you feel helpless against the fierce storm of your circumstances. The wind of the storm knocks you down as dark clouds close in around you.

I've experienced many of these situations and more throughout my lifetime. I thought I'd survived the worst, but then the most turbulent storm hit, and I didn't know if I could stand against the tempest. Our daughter's marriage was falling apart, the children were hurting, and there was nothing I could do but watch as a tsunami crashed in, destroying everything in its path. The pain I felt left me unable to pray, hardly able to breathe. The agony I experienced was more for my daughter and grandchildren than for myself. I could not rise above it.

"Where is God?" I questioned. Everything was going wrong and the surging waves of the storm tossed me around like a toy boat in the bathtub. Every effort to rise above the blast failed as the undertow of hopeless circumstance drew me in.

I sympathized with the disciples in the middle of a storm at sea while Jesus slept at the bottom of the boat. Where was He? Didn't He know we needed Him now if we ever did?

"Suddenly a furious storm came up on the lake, so that the waves swept over the boat. But Jesus was sleeping. The disciples went and woke him, saying, 'Lord, save us! We're going to drown!' He replied, 'You of little faith, why are you so afraid?' Then he got up and rebuked the winds and the waves, and it was completely calm. The men were amazed and asked, 'What kind of man is this? Even the winds and the waves obey him!'" Matthew 8:24-27 (NIV)

Have you ever wondered why they were so amazed, asking: "What kind of a man is this?" They had seen Him perform supernatural healings and deliver the demoniac. Later they experienced being with Him when the dead were raised — but they never reacted as they did here.

My son preached a sermon recently where he brought this question to the forefront. The disciples never reacted this way when He performed other miracles. Why were they not dumbfounded when they witnessed His healing power? My son asked that question in preparing his sermon and felt the

Holy Spirit whispered to him: "Because it was their storm."

You rejoice when someone is healed or receives an answer to an urgent prayer. You're happy for them. But when you are in the storm with no way out — fear is overpowering. It is when your storm is stilled, when your tempest is halted, that you in amazement say, "What manner of man is this?"

He is the storm-stiller. He has promised peace and comfort, and during the storm you can have an assurance from God that He is not asleep — He's in control. It's then, as you praise Him during the difficulties, that fear subsides.

The pain I felt left me unable to pray, hardly able to breathe.

Waiting out the storm in the hollow of His hand, He gives you the strength to endure. The waves of the storm can come crashing over you, but you have shelter in the power of His righteous right hand! He's not only awake, but He holds you fast against the surging storm. He is there; you're not alone no matter how fierce the storm. He has the last word and works for your good.

So, fear not — Jesus is there! At the end of the storm you will look around and wonder why you were so anxious. And if there are shattered pieces around you, He will mend broken hearts and bring healing and restoration where needed. I can testify that He at times has stilled my storm, and at other times has held me close and seen me through the storm. His Word is true; His promises are real.

So, how did I survive the greatest personal storm of my

life? In my darkest hours, I began to see God's hand working through my thirteen-year-old granddaughter. She was suffering the loss of the family life she had always known. I saw her cling to the song "Praise Him in the Storm" by Chris Tomlin. Intrigued with sign language, she entered a Fine Arts competition, signing the song. As she performed with intense emotion, she praised despite her broken home and broken heart. The song became her lifeline and mine.

When the storms of life come — and they will — when you're about to sink, remember Isaiah 43:5, "Do not be afraid, for I am with you." (NIV) This is a solid promise from the Lord. He is still in your boat, during your storm.

The Blame Game

Tifany Trees

"For He Himself has said, 'I will never leave you nor forsake you.'" — *Hebrews 13:5 NKJV*

W hat a terrible mess!"

I've said these words a million times. Most often, I've said it when life has taken a sudden detour and not worked out the way I expected. I usually only have myself to blame for lousing it up, like the time I forgot to confirm my dentist appointment and they canceled it on me. I hold myself accountable though, by vowing to not do whatever it is again or do better next time. But sometimes, when I'm not the cause, I've blamed God. I've blamed Him for the mess when I can't make sense of what is happening.

Like most people, it's hard for me to accept things that just happen, especially something bad. I've often heard the saying, "Everything happens for a reason." Although I believe this to be true, it doesn't make difficult things any more tolerable. But who's to blame when bad things do happen?

Eight years ago when my father was dying of cancer, it wasn't me who caused the tumors to grow in his body that led to his death. Twenty years ago when my husband had an affair and ended our marriage, it wasn't me who didn't show up to the court-ordered counseling sessions. Or this year when my car got hit from behind while I was making a turn, it wasn't my insurance that had to pay the claim. These horrible situations were all out of my control, and they made deep, lasting impacts in my life that rippled through my family. The stress and anxiety from these hardships often made me feel alone, on my own to face the very real loss, pain and suffering, property damage, and even death. Why did God bring these terrible troubles upon me? Where was He in the midst of my sorrows?

Then it hit me. Usually in the middle of throwing a good pity-party, I'm reminded that it is not God who brings troubles into our lives. He is always good and there is no evil in Him. Then who brings trouble? The devil does. The one who is our enemy, the ancient serpent.

Why did God bring these terrible troubles upon me?

He is to blame for the evil running amok everywhere. What's more, he uses times of trouble to hurt us, confuse us, and to get us to take our eyes off God, who is our hope and joy.

We were never promised we wouldn't have troubles in this life, in fact quite the opposite. Jesus told us in John 16:33 (NLT) that "Here on earth you will have many trials and sorrows. But take heart, because I have overcome the world." The apostle Peter warns us that our enemy "prowls around like a roaring lion looking for someone to devour," (1 Peter 5:8 NLT), but he is already defeated! Jesus paid the price with His blood to overcome that crafty serpent!

Our lives may not be tame and quiet, but we will not be

overtaken. Even in times of war, economic collapse, plagues, and pandemonium, when it looks and feels like we're doomed, the enemy will not prevail.

Knowing we would face hard times, our heavenly Father made us a lasting promise, "I will never leave you nor forsake you." That means we never have to face anything alone, no matter what it is, no matter how big or how small or seemingly insignificant. Not only that, He also promised to see us through these hard times. Psalm 34:17 (NKJV) says, "*The righteous* cry out, and the LORD hears, And delivers them out of all their troubles." His timing may seem to cut a little close, but that's how He works sometimes.

Now, in the midst of my troubles, I take great comfort in knowing that He hears my cries for help and is already working on the solution to my problem.

What could be better than the King of the Universe, who is bigger and mightier than any calamity, being at my side during my times of trouble? It's true I cannot physically see Him beside me, but I trust He's there because of His promise. With great love and deep compassion for us, He works behind the scenes to cause even our hardships to be used for our good. What the enemy intended for our defeat, God turns around and uses to prove Himself faithful to us. So even though I can't see Him working on my behalf, I can see the results of His handiwork. In the end, things always work out.

Though God didn't keep my father from dying, or my husband from leaving me, or stop that car from hitting me, His love is evident all around me. His promise produces love, joy, peace, protection, and provision in both times of crisis and times of calm. When I stop myself from focusing on the problem and remember His word to never leave me, I can tangibly feel His peace come over me like a waterfall and cascade into every one of my problems.

No more blaming God for my woes. Rather, I will look up and thank Him for His promise to be with me always and forever.

Tapestries of His Grace

Cheryl Weber

"The LORD is good, A stronghold in the day of trouble;
And He knows those who trust in Him." — Nahum 1:7 NKJV

Years ago as a young single woman, I complained to the Lord that I didn't have a man to take care of me. I strongly sensed him saying, "Cheryl, I can take better care of you than any man ever could."

I am now a middle-aged, single woman and God has been true to that promise.

On a cold, dark night early in November 2014, He reminded me of His faithfulness. It was a little after 9:00. I had just left work and was headed home when an oncoming SUV swerved into my lane. Hardly able to believe my eyes, I yanked my steering wheel to the right, hoping the other driver would correct and avoid a collision.

She didn't. The SUV slammed into my sub-compact sedan. My windshield cracked into spiderwebs of broken glass as airbags deployed into my face. When the dust cleared, I looked out my window. Parts of my front bumper and hood were scattered across the road. There was no sign of movement from the SUV that lay flipped on its side in the other lane.

I shoved against my door in an attempt to get out and check on the other driver. It was jammed, so I fished for my cell phone and called for help. By this time the young woman had climbed out of her vehicle and was sitting on the edge of the road with her phone.

Police cruisers, fire trucks, and ambulances soon arrived. An officer told me the other driver had fallen asleep at the wheel causing her to career into my lane. She'd lost consciousness briefly from the impact so she was whisked away to the hospital. Fire Rescue took at least ten minutes to pry open my door since they didn't want me crawling out the passenger side. I refused treatment since my injuries — one negligible bruise and a minor sprain to my right hand — were not worth a trip to the ER.

I went home to bed but I didn't sleep at all.

I believe it was ultimately God's presence that strengthened and protected me that dark night. Perhaps angels cushioned the impact or the Father's arms embraced me as the two vehicles collided. I thought of Psalm 34:7 that says, "The angel of the LORD encamps all around those who fear Him, And delivers them" (NKJV). Later, I remembered Psalm 94:13 that states, "That You may grant him [power to calm himself and find] peace in the days of adversity" (AMP).

Those sheltering arms reached beyond my immediate need.

Due to various reasons beyond my control, I had no significant savings with which to purchase another vehicle. "Lord, You know I want to save money. But every time I begin, something happens and I have big bills to pay. I've tithed faithfully for years. What is going on? Please work things out so I don't have to shell out any extra money for another car."

I did my part and then watched God do His. The other driver's insurance company gave me about $1000 more for my car than I had expected. My nephew Brad, an excellent mechanic, went on the hunt for another vehicle for me. However, we both got a bit frustrated when he tracked down one likely vehicle after another only to have someone else beat him to it.

After the third possibility fell through I prayed again. "Lord, lead Brad to the car meant just for me."

Then my nephew heard a coworker had a family member who wanted to upgrade to a newer car. The coworker was willing to sell for a bargain price, just to get the previous vehicle out of the way. It needed some work that Brad took care of and when he was finished, I only had to pay a couple hundred dollars rather than months of payments.

After the third possibility fell through I prayed again. "Lord, lead Brad to the car meant just for me."

God had graciously answered my prayer, perhaps not exactly as I had asked, but in a way that still demonstrated His kind provision.

Some situations are not wrapped up as neatly as mine. When we face unbearable heartache and anguish, everything we thought we knew about God and how life should work can be shaken. We are not promised immunity to suffering, yet

Jesus conquered the world for us. (John 16:33) He was a man of sorrows and acquainted with grief, who bore the weight of the world's sin on His perfect shoulders. Our Savior is the One who can rescue us, even in situations that appear impossible.

When we turn our eyes from our own fear and pain and focus on Him, we hear the echoes of His presence and whispers of His grace. These weave themselves like shining strands through our tribulations as He walks beside us, before us, behind us, and lays His hand upon us. Even when we can't discern His presence, He is there and He is busy on our behalf.

Only a Shadow

Deb Kemper

"Yea, though I walk through the valley of the shadow of death, I will fear no evil." — Psalm 23:4 NKJV

You need a colonoscopy," my doctor declared.

"I have two years before I'm sixty," I protested as I dressed over fractured ribs. Nine years in our old house without a level floor, I'd never fallen before.

She shook her head no, then explained something looked suspicious on the blood work from my hip surgery six weeks ago.

"Okay."

"Joyce will call you with the appointment."

A week later, my husband, Ken, and I waited in a small airless room with twenty irritable people. The doctor was running an hour and a half late. I'd fasted for a full day; low blood sugar echoed in a throbbing headache.

Eventually my presence was required.

"I'm sorry we're behind schedule," the nurse said as she adjusted the IV drip line. "We had new equipment installed this morning." She'd had a rough morning.

I smiled and covered my eyes with my forearm. "Need to shake the headache."

"The IV will take a few minutes." She left as another entered.

"Mrs. Kemper?" a deep masculine voice spoke.

"Yes?"

"I'll be handling your procedure this morning."

"Has the requirement changed for colonoscopies from ten years to eight?" I squinted in the glare.

"No, why?"

"My doctor insisted."

"Something's amiss."

"Okay, let's do it."

He nodded. "I'll see you in the procedure room."

Moments later an orderly pushed the gurney down the hallway. I closed my eyes as the anesthesiologist said, "I'll see you in a few minutes."

When I woke from the procedure the doctor was with us in recovery, my husband at hand.

"I found two polyps, one is common, the other can be cancerous. We'll send it for a biopsy. I think it's fine, we caught it early. If we'd done the procedure yesterday I may not have found them. They were in a part of the colon that's very difficult to see because it curves. But now we have a 3-D camera so I saw everything."

"Thank God it was today," Ken answered.

"You'll hear from us when the biopsy comes in."

On Thursday, my doctor called with the results. "The polyp was cancerous."

On Thursday, my doctor called with the results. "The polyp

was cancerous." She paused to give me a moment. "You okay?"

"Trying to get my mind around it."

She talked about seeing an oncologist and a surgeon, then asked again. "You alright?"

"Not as good as I was before you called." I tried to comprehend an alien mutant growing in my body.

"If you need me…"

"I'll be fine."

I called Ken at work. "It's cancer." I tried to sort how the worst thing that can, had happened.

"I'll be home in a few minutes."

Four days later, we sat across the table from the oncologist. "I wish we could catch all of them at stage zero."

"What are our treatment options?" I asked.

We went back and forth and finally settled on seeing a surgeon immediately. Several days later I checked into the hospital. The staff was friendly, the surgical team amazing. I spent three restless days in a small room with no window to open, staring wistfully at the exit below me.

They finally released me with surety that the pathology report looked good. They failed to mention it was only preliminary.

I left in pajama pants that fit over the dressings on my extended belly. Breathing fresh air was good.

Two weeks later, we returned to the surgeon's office for the final report. He had removed seventeen lymph nodes. There were more cancerous cells where they shouldn't have been. The cancer had metastasized and moved through my bloodstream.

The oncologist re-rated the cancer to early stage three. I needed chemotherapy. I cannot eat processed or chemically preserved food without becoming ill. How could I handle chemo?

"You can't even clean with chemicals," our daughter cried.

Our son was flabbergasted. "Mom, I don't know what to say."

"Take time to get used to the idea. We're still working on it."
I comforted him with all the confidence of someone stepping
into a different world — one without oxygen or light.

We chose fewer chemo treatments, having watched too
many peers succumb to the cure rather than the disease. Of
this I was certain, my heavenly Father loved me and knew
what I could endure. He would show my children He was at
work in the madness.

We canceled summer road trips, grandchildren spending
weeks here splashing in the pool, and pulling weeds in our
veggie plot. Instead, Ken tended a smaller garden alone, while
I watched from the window.

Neuropathy made my fingers so sensitive I used oven mitts
to move the milk jug in the fridge. My mouth stayed full of
sores, lips puffy and tender. Everything I drank tasted like dirt.

Through experiencing the results of chemotherapy, my
Lord went ahead of me. He appointed the day new equipment
was in place when I had my colonoscopy. He gave wisdom
to doctors and surgeons. He went behind me to heal damage
caused by the chemotherapy, though a lifetime cannot restore
what has been lost. We live with what we have and count each
day as precious.

Jesus did not promise if we have difficulties. He promised
when we have them, He'll be here to hold our hands. With
every step through this dark valley of cancer, God provided all
I needed to recover. The cancer risk will remain, because once
it occurs and they pump us full of poison, it is likely to happen
again — but it's only a shadow of death.

God's Promise

for our

BASIC NEEDS

*"And Abraham called the name of the place,
The-Lord-Will-Provide; as it is said to this day,
'In the Mount of the Lord it shall
be provided.'" —Genesis 22:14 NKJV*

Order my Steps and Guide my Socks!

Vanessa Burke

"For I was hungry and you gave Me food; I was thirsty and you gave Me drink; I was a stranger and you took Me in; I was naked and you clothed Me; I was sick and you visited Me; I was in prison and you came to Me." — Matthew 25:35-36 NKJV

Some prayers I pray daily, without fail. One of them is "Lord, please establish my thoughts and order my steps." Such promises are in His Word, and we know that God's Word does not return void but accomplishes everything it is meant to (see Isaiah 55:11). I believe His Word, and every day when I pray this prayer, God does just that.

One recent morning, I put on some warm fuzzy purple socks to pounce around the house in. I figured I would change them at some point before going to work. Well, I forgot, and so off I went to work with some slip-on heels without even thinking about the socks. About half way to work, I happened to glance down, and I almost stopped the car as I noticed my loud and glaring purple socks. So I thought, I'll just stop by Walgreen's and get some knee-highs.

Driving down the street, singing to praise music, I hastily turned into what I thought was the driveway for Walgreen's. Instead, it was a closed restaurant. How'd I get here? Just as I was about to drive out of the parking lot, I noticed a homeless woman who seemed to come out of nowhere, and she and I both stopped and stared at each other. I knew in that instant this was a meeting God had gently guided me to. She strolled over to the car as I rolled down the window.

"Are you hungry?" I asked her. As she nodded, I proceeded to give her most of what I had packed for my lunch.

"Are you a God person?" She was so excited.

"Yes, ma'am, I am." Then I asked if she knew God loved her.

"Oh yeah. I'm still alive."

I then steered the conversation to the Bible, specifically Romans 10:9: "if you confess with your mouth the Lord Jesus and believe in your heart that God has raised Him from the dead, you will be saved." (NKJV)

"Oh, I know all about that." She continued speaking, mentioning her brother who was really beat up and bruised. It was uncanny the way she talked about how her brother suffered, almost as if this brother she spoke about was Jesus Himself, as He also suffered greatly, beaten and bruised before carrying that heavy piece of wood we call the cross.

Since she knew all about Romans 10:9, I asked had she actually done what it said.

"You bet!" We had a good laugh.

"I'm thirsty. Have anything to drink?" she said as she ate.

I had two water bottles, both less than half empty. I poured one into the other and gave it to her. Her grin widened. The conversation then turned to clothing.

"You got a lot of clothes," she stated emphatically. "Don't you? I need some clothes; I'm freezing."

I looked around in the car and wouldn't you know it, I had packed some workout clothes for later that evening, so I handed her the bag and informed her she now had a new T-shirt, pants, and socks. At the word *pants* she lit up like a five-year-old, which made my heart smile.

With the biggest grin, she declared God had blessed her that day. I asked if I could read some of His Word to her. So we read a little. She asked me for a third time if I had any Christian literature, which delightfully surprised me. She seemed as eager to have the literature about God as much as the food, water, and clothing. I was so enjoying meeting Gigi.

I'm so grateful He guides our footsteps, even when we're wearing purple socks.

As a parting word, I told her that Jesus said, "Assuredly, I say to you, inasmuch as you did *it* to one of the least of these My brethren, you did *it* to Me." (Matthew 25:40 NKJV) I explained that everything I had given her, I was really giving to Jesus. At that, she closed her eyes and felt it for a moment… and she had the most peaceful countenance. She asked for a hug and I obliged. Yes, she was dirty, and her hair badly needed a wash, but in that moment that didn't matter. I knew Jesus would have given her a hug, too. In fact, He did… through me.

The Holy Spirit didn't want me to change my purple socks that morning. He needed to bless one of His children, and already had an encounter planned for me and Gigi.

When you find yourself in a strange place, don't always be in such a hurry to leave. Stop, assess your surroundings, and consider the possibility that you may be just where God wants you. He may be using you to provide Him food, something to drink, and clothing for His journey — a journey He takes every day as He walks with, and sometimes carries, His precious children.

I'm so grateful He guides our footsteps, even when we're wearing purple socks.

God and the Small Details

Renita F. Gerlach

"Every good and perfect gift is from above, coming down from the Father of the heavenly lights, who does not change like shifting shadows." — James 1:17 NIV

What do a large purple exercise ball and a twenty-inch over-the-door basketball hoop have in common? Both are objects God used to show He knows and cares about the small details in my life.

My husband and I home educate our three children. Since a large portion of their day is spent at home, we are always looking for ways to keep bodies active while engaging the mind, especially inside during the winter months. Living on one income, we can't go out and buy everything we want in order to set up the perfect schoolroom, so we have to be creative in our purchases. Yet over the years, our Jehovah-Jireh has shown Himself faithful to provide what we need.

When my oldest was nine, our family attended an event at a local Christian ministry that uses a barbecue chicken restaurant to provide food, Bible teaching, and discipleship training for their community. Although we thoroughly enjoyed our experience, the most impactful thing we received that day was a free home exercise kit, given out by the dozen to those who attended. Included was an exercise ball with a pump. When I took it home and inflated it, the huge ball immediately attracted my children's attention.

Over the six years since then I have seen more uses of that ball than I could have ever imagined.

My son bounced it or bounced on it while he said his spelling words aloud. He sat on it, rolling around in circles to stay focused when he had to listen. My daughter used it on top of a chair as a throne while we sat together for group activities. The children pushed or kicked it back and forth in a big open space during indoor recess. I perched on it during hours and hours of read aloud so I could stay alert and tone my abs — multi-tasking at its best!

Somewhere along the line, I realized how important this ball was in our home school. So when we had it out on the deck one spring day and a vigorous bounce sent it sailing over the railing where it landed on a sharp yucca plant and popped, that was a sad day! And a replacement ball quickly made its way to the top of the Christmas list that year.

The first ball was free, provided by God, an unlikely item I

"Bargain shopping bingo! Masterminded by a loving heavenly Father for His children."

never would have thought to purchase for our schoolroom. Another item God provided on a trip to the local thrift store. I paid $2 for a Spalding NBA Slam Jam Over-the-door Mini Basketball Hoop, sold on Amazon for $30. Bargain shopping bingo! Masterminded by a loving heavenly Father for His children.

That hoop, fastened over a wooden beam crossing our great room's middle, has consistently provided many a boy or girl with indoor action and exercise. Family games of knockout get even Mom and Dad involved in blood pressure-raising, adrenaline-pumping, laughter-bubbling activity. The hoop draws friends in like a magnet when they arrive to visit. A son and two daughters create challenge throws where they attempt long shots from the bottom of the steps or the lower level playroom to try to make baskets, difficult but not impossible.

So this purple ball and indoor hoop engage and keep active three homeschool students, meeting a need their teacher didn't even fully realize they had at first. This shows a Father God at work who knows our needs even before we ask.

What is your need right now? Where is the place in your life that feels lacking? God knows and sees. He is El Roi, the God who sees, as a mistreated woman named Hagar discovered in Genesis 16. God loves you. He has promised to supply all your needs through Christ Jesus (Philippians 4:19), and to do exceedingly abundantly above all you ask or think (Ephesians 3:20). He is the God who gives every good and perfect gift (James 1:17).

My life is not perfect. I am heartbroken by things that happen to and within myself and those I love. Yet when I am discouraged, I call to mind God's promises, which are "yes" in Christ Jesus. I recollect that God is good, and I list the things He has done for me. Among other things, I remember a purple ball and an over-the-door basketball hoop.

And my heart rejoices!

Five Casseroles and a Prayer

Sally Jadlow

"Then He commanded the multitudes to sit down on the grass. And He took the five loaves and the two fish, and looking up to heaven, He blessed and broke and gave the loaves to the disciples; and the disciples gave to the multitudes. So they all ate and were filled, and they took up twelve baskets full of the fragments that remained. — Matthew 14:19-20 NKJV

Five hostesses gathered in the church kitchen for the final preparation for our monthly Women's Association luncheon. Each of us brought a 9-by-12 casserole, complete with vegetables and chicken — more than enough for our usual group of thirty to thirty-five women.

I glanced up from my station in the kitchen and gasped. "Oh my goodness! Where are all these people coming from? Are they all here for our luncheon?"

My friend let out a short laugh. "I told you this speaker would be popular. Let's get out there and set up some more tables."

We didn't stop until we made room for eighty guests —

twice the number we dared to expect. The cooks gathered in the kitchen for an emergency conference. I glanced out the serving window. Our guests filled every available seat.

"What are we going to do? I thought we would have plenty," Barb said.

"It's 12:00," Mimi said as she looked at her watch. "It's too late to go get some lettuce to make a salad or buy some rolls to help stretch it. This is a disaster."

"Well," B.J. said and giggled, "I guess we could pray and ask the Lord to multiply the food like He did for the 5,000."

While the president blessed the meal in the fellowship hall, we prayed in the kitchen for Jesus to help us — now.

The ladies formed a line at the window. B.J. picked up the serving spoon and dished out the chicken and vegetable casserole on each plate.

My heavens. She'd better not give such generous portions. We'll run out for sure before everyone is served. I opened my mouth to encourage her to make smaller portions but saw the end of the line near the serving window. What if someone wants seconds? The hostesses better not eat, just in case someone comes back.

Just then B.J. made an announcement. "Ladies, if anyone wants seconds we have plenty."

What in the world possessed her to say such a thing? I couldn't watch any longer. I left the kitchen and slipped into a seat at a table in the back of the room.

"Did your circle make these casseroles?" one lady asked. "They're delicious. I think I'll have some more."

"Me too," said the person sitting beside her.

Before the speaker began, almost everyone went back for more. Somehow it stretched, thank God.

After the meeting, the hostesses headed for the kitchen

to clean up.

"I thought we were going to run out for sure."

"I never saw casseroles stretch so far."

"We must have come out even. This last pan is scraped clean," Mimi said.

Barb put the last casserole in the dishwater and looked across the kitchen. "Where did that one come from?"

I never saw casseroles stretch so far.

"What one?" Bunny asked.

"There. Under the tea towel. Didn't we have five casseroles?"

"One, two, three, four…" Mimi counted the clean casseroles on the dish drainer. "How could we have served all those people on four casseroles?"

We looked at each other in a hushed awe and then exploded in laughter. God had indeed answered our prayers.

We divided the remaining casserole into five portions and each hostess took a portion home for dinner that night for our families — another twenty people in all.

"That's a good casserole. Thanks, Mom!" my son said after dinner. I chuckled. Little did he know what a heavenly dish we all enjoyed.

I wonder how many blessings we miss because we fail to ask.

The Stranger

Barbara Latta

"Freely you have received; freely give." — Matthew 10:8 NIV

It was July and the drought we were experiencing in the south had dried the vegetation to an extra crispy dull brown. Temperatures were breaking records as the mercury in thermometers rose higher every day with no relief in the forecast. The sky shone clear blue, usually a welcome sight, but some clouds full of rain would have been summer's gift to a thirsty ground and parched air.

My son and I were traveling from our home in Georgia to visit my parents in Arkansas. We stopped for gas about halfway through the trip. I got out to stretch my legs while my son pumped gas into our vehicle. I could see heat rising off the pavement in waves as I stepped out of my vehicle. The car's air conditioner had been working overtime, and I was anxious to get back into that coolness as quickly as possible. I turned around and saw a woman walk toward us from the other side of the parking lot.

"Excuse me, but I was wondering if you could spare a little money?" she asked me. She was twisting her hands as she looked at the ground while she spoke.

There were others at the gas pumps so I don't know why she chose us, unless she had already asked someone else and received no response. Her hair was disheveled and her blouse was drenched in sweat.

"I'm still three hours away from where I'm going and I've run out of gas," she told me. She had been at this station for hours and was losing hope of getting any help.

There is always room for skepticism when a stranger approaches asking for money, and my first thoughts were about brushing her off in case she was just trying to scam people out of money. But I had been asking God to show me how to help others more, and this looked like an answer to that prayer and a test to see if I would obey.

As my son filled her tank, I knew they needed more than fuel for the car.

"Where's your vehicle?" I asked.

Her hand shook as she pointed to an older model hatchback parked next to the curb. Three little dirty, sweaty faces peered across the parking lot at me as their bodies hung out the windows watching the exchange. A little boy opened the car door and started running toward where we were standing. The mother hurried back to catch the child before he ran in front of a car that was trying to get to a gas pump. The children's voices were getting louder, and they kept asking why they couldn't get out of the vehicle. The smallest one began to cry.

I felt God's hand urging me to help this family. I couldn't leave a woman and small children stranded. I had been stranded before and knew what it felt like.

I walked over to the car as she was trying to calm the children and asked, "Do you have enough gas left to make it to the pump?"

She nodded and got behind the wheel and moved the car over next to mine. As my son filled her tank, I knew they needed more than fuel for the car.

I saw those children sitting in the sun and knew if the mother couldn't buy gas, she probably couldn't buy food either. I could almost hear their stomachs growling, so I went inside and purchased some sandwiches, milk, and water.

"God's hand was in this meeting," I said as I handed the food to the mother. "He loves you and He is providing for you and the kids."

She bit her lip and nodded in agreement, unable to speak as she held back tears. I gave her a little bit of money before she left in case she needed more as she traveled.

"Thank you," she said.

This woman, whom I had never met before and probably will never see again, met a need in me as much as I was able to meet hers. God's blessings flow through people. He blesses us so we can be a blessing to others, not so we can hoard the things He gives us. There were several gas stations at this exit. We could have chosen any of them, but God led us to this one where an opportunity for sharing awaited us.

Every time I see someone on the side of the road I think about this stranger whose very presence provided a way for me to bring God's love and goodness to her. I am always listening to see if another stranded person is someone for me to bless. As I think of this family, I see those children's faces and their mother's hopelessness in my mind and hope and pray that the provision given to them that day will stay with them in the coming years to remind them that God is watching over and taking care of them.

He freely gave so I could freely give. And I am so blessed in return. God provided for two families that day. Mine and hers.

A Place to Call Home

Tynea Lewis

"Now to him who is able to do immeasurably more than all we ask or imagine, according to his power that is at work within us." — Ephesians 3:20 NIV

When my husband and I got married, we found a place to rent just weeks before our wedding, but I had my heart set on owning a house. That's what I expected we would do when we got married… not rent. And how long were we going to be in a place that wasn't ours? It couldn't be that long. We belonged in a house. I felt we deserved a place that was our own.

A year and a half went by, and we still didn't find a place to call our own, but something else came up. My grandpa bought a house at auction and wondered if we would be willing to rent it. Sure. That sounded good. Sharing walls with another family was less than ideal, so I loved the idea of having a house that was our own. Even though it didn't belong to us, it felt a little more like home.

Six months later my grandfather decided to sell the house,

so we had to move again. By this time, we had a baby on the way, so I wanted to settle down before we were moving baby items along with our own. I really wanted a place that was ours. Now more than ever.

Where were we going to live? During the previous two years, we had spent most Sunday afternoons going from open house to open house, but the search became more frantic in the months leading up to our daughter's birth. The number of houses we walked through continued to pile up, but we didn't find anything. If I loved it, my husband found something wrong with it. If he loved it, I didn't want to live in that area. It seemed like we were never going to find anything.

As God always does, He blew my mind with what He had in store.

Why was God not providing a house for us? We did everything we could to find something, but it seemed like there was one letdown after another. With a baby on the way, we needed to find something, but I didn't want to settle. I didn't want to end up somewhere just because we had to.

I expected God to provide us with the perfect house to purchase. I thought it was our time for that, but He had something else in mind.

My parents decided to have my grandmother move in with them, which left her house empty. And it wasn't just any house. It was the house I lived in from birth through fifth grade — my childhood home. My parents thought it would be a great idea for us to move in and rent from them. Was I really going to get to move back to the house that held all of my childhood memories? That wasn't on my radar. I expected a new place, a place that didn't have any memories.

As God always does, He blew my mind with what He had in store. I was going to get to raise my family in the woods, a place I loved to explore as a child. God was going to give my daughter a chance to make the same kind of incredible memories.

Now I understood why all those other houses had something wrong with them. They were not the place God planned for us to live.

Were we still renting? Yes, but the rent was cheaper than any other place we lived, giving us the flexibility for me to leave my teaching job to raise our children. If we had bought a place, the outcome to this all could have been very different. What a blessing God had in store for us even through all the frustration.

Sometimes we want something so specific we fail to see the amazing things God has planned instead. His plan is always better than the best plan we could construct. What disappointment in your life could actually be God preparing something better for you? Open your heart to the possibility.

Why I Memorize Scripture

Arlene Lila

"This Book of the Law shall not depart from your mouth, but you shall meditate on it day and night, that you may observe to do according to all that is written in it. For then you will make your way prosperous, and then you will have good success." Joshua 1:8 NKJV

In giving us His Word, our heavenly Father made provision for our many needs. Learning this some forty years ago, I began to memorize Bible verses and passages on a daily basis. Like having my cell phone within reach and ready to use in an instant, I put God's Word in my brain for immediate use. God's instructions are precious to me. I want to have access to His thoughts at any given moment.

People ask me why I've been memorizing Scripture for so many years. Here are a few reasons why it is crucial to me.

Our heavenly Father admonishes me to hide his Word in my heart.

In the words of the verse above, God tells us to spend time meditating on His Word. I take this as a command, not merely a suggestion.

As we read the Psalms, we see that King David took God's Word seriously. He said, "Your word have I hidden in my heart, That I might not sin against You." (Psalm 119:11 NKJV)

I cannot think of a better way to spend an allotted time than hiding God's Word in my heart.

To bring comfort to others.

My best friend in childhood was Delores. For the eight years of grade school we were very close. But after graduation we attended different high schools. A Christmas card arrived in the mail over the next twenty years, but nothing more.

When a letter came from Delores, the news that she had suffered from severe depression for years saddened me. Doctors and medicine gave no relief. "What can I do to comfort her?" I wondered. Comforting verses I had memorized came to my mind. In a return letter I included a verse from Psalms. "O my soul, why be so gloomy and discouraged? Trust in God! I shall again praise him for his wondrous help; he will make me smile again, *for he is my God!*" (Psalm 43:5 TLB)

In the many letters between us, I always wrote a comforting verse. She later said she read them over and over. Months after we began to correspond, a blood clot formed in her leg and lodged in her heart. I would miss her, but had wonderful memories of our childhood.

Two months passed and I received a phone call from her husband. He said he was cleaning out Delores' things from her closet and bedside table and discovered she had saved all my letters. "They must have meant a lot to her!" he said.

It was God's Word that made her save the letters. I know that now. If I had not memorized those verses, I would not have written them. Those verses from a year's correspondence provided her the comfort she needed. Especially during the last few months of her life.

It gives confidence in witnessing.

On an airline trip, I sat next to a young woman who told me about living with her boyfriend.

"What do you think about that?" I asked her.

"Oh, I think it's wonderful to know you can get along before marriage!" After a long pause, she asked, "What do you think about it?"

"I hate it because God hates it."

"How do you know God hates it?"

"Because it says so in the Bible," I replied.

"I read the whole Bible and there is no place where it says you can't live together," she retorted.

I just wanted to go to bed, cry, and pity myself.

I pointed out to her that the Bible says a lot about it. Whenever you see the word fornication. Her mouth dropped open like I told her she had cancer.

"Read about it in the book of Ephesians," I suggested. "It's in chapter five."

The young lady had many more questions after that, and by the time we landed, she affirmed she needed to make some changes.

It gave me comfort in my time of grieving.

When my husband passed away a few years ago, depression stalked me like an unwanted visitor. I knew I had to fight it and God's Word helped me. I began to sing praise songs and songs of worship when I felt so alone. I walked around the house with a song on my lips when I least felt like doing it. I just wanted to go to bed, cry, and pity myself. However, God's Word provided a way to victory. I learned from the Scriptures exactly what I needed to do. "The garment of praise for the spirit of heaviness." (Isaiah 61:3 NKJV)

It's exciting to know the promise God gives us as a reward if we memorize Scripture: "For then you will make your way prosperous, and then you will have good success." (Joshua 1:8 NKJV)

What a promise! How can I not take seriously the hiding of God's Word in my heart?

Thank you, Lord for giving us Your Word so we can see all the things You have provided for us.

It Just So Happened

Nancy Ruegg

"Before they call I will answer; while they are still speaking I will hear." — Isaiah 65:24 NIV

I just got off the phone with Mary," Frieda began, her words tumbling out in a hurry. "You are not going to believe this."

Frieda was chairperson for the parsonage committee of our church. The congregation had just purchased a newer home, closer to the church, for their clergy family. My husband was their pastor.

Because the new house was also larger, some furniture would be required. (Until about ten years ago, parsonages of our denomination were supposed to be furnished.) Frieda had called to tell me about an interesting development.

While chatting with Mary, our choir director, Frieda just happened to mention the committee was shopping for parsonage furniture.

"Well, I've got a whole storage unit full of furniture, and I need to sell it!" Mary said.

"What do you have?" Frieda inquired.

The more items Mary listed, the more excited Frieda became: a dining room table and four chairs, a matching buffet, a bedroom set, and curio cabinet — furniture that *just happened* to match a number of items on our shopping list.

"It's all in very good condition, too," Mary affirmed. "I just don't have room for it in my current place."

Within a day or two, Frieda and I visited the storage unit with Mary. As we carefully unstacked various pieces for a better look, my eyes grew wide with delight.

"These pieces will blend perfectly with what we already have," I exclaimed.

He's the one doing the orchestrating.

The furniture, traditional in style, appeared in excellent condition. Much of it was off-white, which suited our Florida climate. The dining table had a dark wood top and white legs — very attractive. Generous Mary was more than fair on the price of it all. That left extra dollars in our limited budget for other expenditures.

If only there were six dining chairs instead of four, I thought. Four seats for a family of five meant we'd always be pulling out the folding chairs to accommodate guests.

That's okay, I told myself. Be thankful for the lovely furniture you already have. But I mentioned my wish to Frieda, and she suggested we check a few thrift stores for two more dining chairs. "Maybe we'll find a couple that at least coordinate with Mary's set. If you put them on the ends, the combination could actually look planned."

At the third or fourth store, while scanning the tightly

packed furniture, I spotted two chairs that didn't just co-ordinate with Mary's — they *just so happened* to be almost identical. My jaw dropped.

"Can you believe this?" I exclaimed. "The only obvious difference is the seat covers!"

"Well, that's easy to fix," Frieda announced gleefully. "We'll get them all reupholstered!"

Once the chairs were covered, a person would have to look very carefully to notice any difference among the chairs.

No doubt, you have some *just-so-happened* stories of your own. Isn't it delightful to be at just the right place at the right time to enjoy such coincidences? Actually, in a universe under control of God Almighty, such events are much more than coincidence; they're God-incidents. *He's* the one doing the orchestrating. Scripture tells us: "Before they call I will answer; while they are still speaking I will hear." (Isaiah 65:24 NIV)

Jesus taught the same truth: "Your Father knows what you need before you ask him." (Matthew 6:8 NIV)

In addition, the Bible is full of examples:

The Egyptian princess *just happened* to find Moses in the bulrushes and saved his life (Exodus 2).

The Israelite spies *just happened* to meet Rahab, a woman willing to help them escape Jericho's authorities (Joshua 2).

Ruth *just happened* to choose Boaz' field for gleaning (Ruth 2).

David *just happened* to be a marksman with a slingshot when Goliath and the Philistines threatened Israel (1 Samuel 17).

Esther *just happened* to be chosen queen of Persia, as Haman was plotting to annihilate the Jews (Esther 2).

Our all-knowing, ever-watchful God foresees each need. And before we're even aware of what's around the corner, He is already there. He has already supplied. Often, it is far beyond what we've asked for or even thought of. Countless times He has engineered events for our benefit. In actuality, those occasions when we recognize His handiwork are probably just a small sampling of the numerous times He has supernaturally provided, protected, and guided.

What a gracious, faithful God He is!

Exactly as Asked

A.D. Shrum

"I will remember the deeds of the LORD;
yes, I will remember your miracles of
long ago." — Psalm 77:11 (NIV)

Ancient Israel had a practice of erecting Ebenezer stones that memorialized an occasion in which God showed up in a big way. You see this after the Lord takes His people across the Jordan River in Deuteronomy 27 and after God grants His people yet another victory against the Philistines in 1 Samuel 7. As the descendants of these people looked back on the memorials, they would be reminded of God's awesome power and His very real involvement.

I think it's a great idea, and because of it, I've taken some black and white pictures and hung them in my bedroom. Each represents a significant event in which the Lord has undeniably shown up in our lives. Among the half dozen photos, I can remember how the Lord miraculously brought my wife to Mayumba, or how He carried us through a life-threatening complication after she gave birth to our son. But of the pictures, one reminds me not only of God's provision, but also His sense of humor.

In the spring of 2006, I was quickly approaching college graduation, but without any job offers. Though I'd been told Mechanical Engineering was a highly employable field, it seemed my prospects weren't any better than anyone else's. I prayed God would allow me to land a job sometime before I graduated, and I busted my tail off do my part.

My parents had graciously offered their home as a place for me to stay if I couldn't find anything. But I was pursuing a young lady at the time, and living in my parents' basement without a job seemed like a huge turnoff. If anything, the offer motivated me to redouble my efforts.

In that semester alone, I applied to well over sixty companies. My initial search was limited to opportunities near my home of Maryland or my alma mater of Virginia Tech, but before long it became a national search, with companies as far as San Antonio receiving my résumé.

Every time the phone rang with an unknown number, I felt a thrill of hope. Then, like now, it was usually just a wrong number, but every now and then it was one of my prospects. In the end, I interviewed with twelve different companies in those five months. Of those twelve, I netted three follow-up interviews on-site. By late March, my confidence peaked. But as March became April, and April approached May, I started to wonder if I'd have anything lined up before turning my tassel.

The last days of school finished, and finals came and went. I hadn't stopped praying God would grant me an offer, nor had I stopped looking, but I had pretty much resigned myself to being a jobless basement dweller for a while.

At last, the day of commencement arrived. I woke up feeling a little disappointed, but decided to celebrate graduation regardless of the status of my employment. Sometime after breakfast that morning, I got a call from an unknown number. But my excitement died when I realized it was just my parents calling from the hotel. They were on their way over to my apartment. I hung up and washed the breakfast dishes as I waited. At ten that morning, I got another call. Didn't recognize it either, but with my roommates' parents staying in hotels as well, I wasn't too hopeful.

"Is this Mr. Alexander Shrum?" a woman asked.

"Yes, who is this?"

She answered with her name and then got right to business. "I'm from General Electric in Greenville, South Carolina, and I'd like to make you a job offer."

I paced the townhouse as she went over salary figures. The numbers made my head spin and I agreed to the terms right away (my coworkers later chastised me for not bargaining for a higher starting pay, but I'd never read that far in the job search books). When my parents arrived, I told them the good news. We laughed, celebrated, and then tried to figure out where Greenville, South Carolina was. The pride in my dad's voice was the icing on the cake. Though secretly, I think he was also glad not to have me living under the house.

He answered my prayer for sure, I just didn't expect Him to cut it so close.

A scant few hours later, I had my diploma in hand. As I sat among my fellow students, I reflected on my prayer that

God would grant me a job before I graduated. He answered my prayer for sure, I just didn't expect Him to cut it so close.

Now whenever I look at the picture of my first business card up on the wall, I have to smile. God always answers prayers on His terms, but sometimes He'll answer a prayer exactly as you asked, even if it isn't exactly what you meant.

We all have stories like this. We just need to be aware of God's hand in our circumstances. You don't have to print out black and white pictures to memorialize your God events, but take time this month to set up a way of reminding yourself of God's past provision — and put it somewhere you'll see often. Then when disaster strikes, you can immediately bring to mind those miracle moments, praising Him for His past provision, and knowing He will provide in the future.

The Roof Over Our Heads

RJ Thesman

"I cling to you; your right hand upholds me." — Psalm 63:8 NIV

When the ink dried on the divorce settlement, my prayer for my son and me was twofold: God, please don't ever let us be homeless. Keep a roof over our heads. And God, please let us have enough food. Don't ever let my son be hungry.

As a biblical counselor who worked with single moms, I knew the stats. The number one demographic living in poverty — anywhere in the world — is the single mom and her children. As a woman who had spent a lifetime in the career field of ministry, I had precious little financial resources to begin this single mom journey.

But I knew God was faithful. I knew His powerful right hand would uphold us.

After I sold the divorce house, a woman I had once mentored came to me and said, "My husband and I are buying some investment property, a townhome. We'd like you and your son to live there — at our cost — with no move-in deposit. You can have pets and you can paint or decorate it to please you."

With grateful hearts, we moved into a beautiful new townhome that allowed us to heal. I stenciled a border of trailing vines that helped me stay focused on abiding in the Vine. I set up my writing desk in a perfect nook with a huge window where I looked out at the cerulean Kansas sky and worshiped the God who supplied our every need.

Friends brought us groceries, huge boxes of canned goods, potatoes, and cereals that filled our pantry for months. Another friend shopped garage sales and discovered décor that repeated the vine theme in every room. We felt surrounded by the truth of John 15 and upheld by God's personal care. Coupons and checks came in the mail, providing extra funds that added a supplemental income for my stretched budget.

Coupons and checks came in the mail, providing extra funds...

A group of women helped me bless the house by praying through each room, then ended with a pizza party — paid for by their generous hearts. These were the same women who once attended my Bible study in the divorce house. Their kindness was a reminder that what we sow, we will someday reap.

On the outside patio, I placed my lawn chair and watched as the homeowner planted several gardens where young trees grew and shrubs began to thrive. I planted my own container gardens that added color and texture each spring and gladdened my heart with the passing of time. The view of God's creation from my patio helped hasten the healing process.

My son set up his guitar and drums, invited friends over to jam, and banged out his emotions to the rhythm of his inner voice. On the piano downstairs, I played the soothing tunes of Mozart and Chopin while occasionally beating out the octaves of Rachmaninoff so that my anger found a place to fuel its fortissimo.

On the front porch, I placed my glider, a gift from in-laws whom I loved and a reminder of better times. A pot of pansies colored one arm of the glider and provided the perfect respite for scribbling in my journal.

Coupons continued to arrive. We often used the buy one/get one burger meals at Sonic for our Tuesday night picnics. A friend and her daughter brought us a pizza we could stick in the oven. Another friend who was a gourmet cook, brought us meals with enough leftovers to keep us eating for a week while her chocolate fudge kept my mood elevated and antioxidants high.

In those days, we did not buy organic because the game was on for survival rather than health. But friends who grew gardens shared with us, and fresh veggies helped us make it through spring, summer, and fall. One pumpkin provided fiber and vitamin K for various recipes. Several green tomatoes became a tangy salsa for ballgame chips and dip.

We never lacked the basic necessities of shelter and food because God was faithful to provide and to send His saints to help us. Either He worked a miracle by whispering instructions to someone, or He let me sell an article to a publication, which provided extra funds.

Even when I was downsized out of my job, God opened doors for temp work and more writing gigs that paid the bills and reminded me once again that abiding in the Vine was the best choice for my redesigned life.

God cares for the orphan and the widow — those who are abandoned either by death or by choice. His merciful heart provides for the wounded so they can heal in peace and comfort even while He deals with the daily needs of life.

Throughout those early years of post-divorce, I kept a journal of answered prayers. Every time, God showed up and provided what we needed.

In the process of caring for our needs, God also taught us it was okay to trust and kept us from straying into the bitterness of soul and lethargy of spirit. Because we knew if He could keep a roof over our heads and food on the table, then we could also trust Him with our hearts.

Contributors

MELODY BALTHASER lives in rural Pennsylvania with her husband and their three children. She enjoys traveling, hiking, camping, and canoeing, and in winter enjoys a classic chick-flick on the TV while homemade soup simmers on the stove. Melody's passion is to encourage people to let God's love free them of fear and rejection so they can live the life their Creator intended. — MelodyBalthaser.com

KELLY F. BARR lives in Lancaster County, Pennsylvania, with her husband, three sons, and their black Labrador retriever. She became interested in writing in the fifth grade and became determined to write in the seventh grade. Kelly is a member of Lancaster Christian Writers and American Christian Fiction Writers and does freelance writing. She has been blogging for over six years. — KellyFBarr.com

CATHERINE ULRICH BRAKEFIELD is an ardent lover of Christ, as well as a hopeless romantic and patriot. She skillfully intertwines these elements into her novels, *Wilted Dandelions* and the upcoming *Destiny Awaits*. Catherine enjoys horse-back riding, swimming, camping, and traveling the byroads across America with Edward, her husband of more than forty years. — CatherineUlrichBrakefield.com

DEBRA L. BUTTERFIELD

MASON K. BROWN moves between her homes in Seaside and Forest Grove, Oregon, with her rescue dog, Wicket. An author, speaker, and storyteller, she writes primarily inspirational non-fiction and humor with a smattering of fiction tossed in. She is widely published in anthologies and devotionals. Visit Mason's website at masonkbrown.com

MARILYN BURELL and her husband, Robert, have been married fifty-eight years and have four married children, nine grandchildren, and one great grandchild. Marilyn is the author of *Raising My Ebenezer Stones*. She prays her stories will inspire others to rise above circumstances and discover a fresh awareness of who God is and thank Him with a grateful heart for His faithfulness.

DEBRA L. BUTTERFIELD is a freelance writer, editor, speaker, and writing coach, and an editor with CrossRiver Media Group. Prior to freelancing, she worked for Focus on the Family as a junior copywriter. She the author of *Carried by Grace* and has contributed to numerous writing projects. Debra enjoys the outdoors and has three adult children and two grandchildren. DebraLButterfield.com

VANESSA BURKE is a skilled editor, writer, and proofreader, experienced in print, digital, social, and corporate communications. Having served as Editor in Chief of Atlanta area magazines, she has published many articles and written devotionals for StreamingFaith.com and advertising industry blog posts for JWT Atlanta. Twitter.com/vanessaburke and About.me/VanessaBurke.

LAURE COVERT is a freelance writer, home-schooling mom, and Spanish interpreter who juggles many life passions. More than twenty-five years of marriage to her husband, Glenn, a Christian counselor who handles the tough cases within their Christian community, have taught Laure that sometimes life is hard, but God is always good. BlueBirdsAlwaysFly.wordpress.com

TRACY CRUMP has written devotionals and articles for *Focus on the Family, ParentLife,* and *Mature Living* and was a columnist for *Southern Writers Magazine,* but storytelling is her passion. More than eighteen of her stories have appeared in Chicken Soup for the Soul books and other anthologies. Tracy enjoys teaching writers through her Write Life Workshops and webinars. WriteLifeWorkshops.com

THERESA JENNER GARRIDO attended the University of Washington, received a B.A. in English, and spent the next twenty-plus years teaching middle school language arts, drama, and social studies before retiring early to devote more time to her writing. She enjoys traveling, visiting friends and family, and poking her nose into strange and mysterious places. BooksByTheresaJGarrido.com

RENITA F. GERLACH is active in the home school arena: educating her children, teaching writing to high school homeschoolers, evaluating students, and leading a home school support group. She replenishes her energy tank by reading, hiking new trails both alone and with her family, baking artisan bread, and interacting with international exchange students.

BARBARA GORDON lives with her husband of thirty-eight years in a small town in west-central Missouri. Their family includes three grown sons, three daughters-in-law, and three precious grandchildren. Barbara retired from a public school system where she was a district administrator. Her days are now filled with babysitting grandchildren and hobbies, which include reading, geocaching, and jogging.

NANCY KAY GRACE is the author of *The Grace Impact*, a devotional about God's grace in everyday life. She is a speaker, Bible teacher, and internet radio host of *Living Life Unedited*. Nancy and her husband, Rick, have served in pastoral ministry for over forty years. They enjoy the stage of life of welcoming grandchildren to the family. NancyKayGrace.com

MERRIE HANSEN and her husband of forty years have called seven different states home. From these many adventures as a wife, mother, grandmother... singer, backpacker, roller-skater, homeschool mom, volunteer... come devotionals to challenge, encourage, and inspire others to Live-Out-Loud-for-Jesus. Some of her work can be found in *The Secret Place*, *Just Between You & Me*, and *The Benefit Package*. MerrieHansen.com.

LONDA HAYDEN is a native Texan now happily living in Tennessee with her husband and three sons. As the founding president of Bartlett Christian Writers, she helps organize workshops and retreats encouraging writers to hone their skills. She is also a staff writer for *Southern Writers Magazine*. Her published works include *Date, Pray, Wait*; *Candy Moon*; and several anthologies. LondaHayden.com

DR. JEAN McLACHLAN HESS, a native of Glasgow, Scotland, has been involved in ministry for over thirty years. A graduate of Glasgow University, she earned a Doctor of Ministry from Denver Seminary in 2007. Jean leads retreats and workshops on prayer and spiritual direction. Jean's Celtic Advent Devotional Book has become a favorite of many. JeanMclachlanHess.com

SANDRA HICKMAN is an Australian author, writer, poet, and songwriter. She served as a missionary in Africa, India, and China; is an evangelist, church leader, intercessory prayer leader. She is the Australian Headquarters ministry leader and staff writer for the Lamp Newsletter in Detroit. She aims to publish her first book, *The Letter*. sandrevival@yahoo.com.au facebook.com/sandra.hickman.503

SALLY JADLOW has authored several books including *God's Little Miracle Book I, II*, and *III*; *The Late Sooner, The Late Sooner's Daughter, Hard Times in the Heartland, Daily Walk with Jesus, Looking Deeper*, and *Family Favorites from the Heartland*. All are available on Amazon in paperback and e-reader. She lives in the Kansas City area with her husband and serves as a chaplain to corporations.

DEB KEMPER, a displaced Southerner, now resides with the love of her life in Lexington, Missouri, a peaceful place with four National Historic Districts and a Civil War Battlefield. Her books range from contemporary Christian fiction to historical fantasy. She is currently writing a gluten-free cookbook, and holds two classes a week for writers already contracted with CDP, her publishing company. DebKemper.com

BARBARA LATTA has a passion to share how the grace of God can free us from the rules of religious tradition. Her writing has been published in several newspapers, magazines, and websites. She enjoys riding motorcycles with her Harley husband and their biker travels are the inspiration for her blog, Navigating Life's Curves. BarbaraLatta. blogspot.com.

TYNEA LEWIS, an elementary teacher turned work-from-home mom of two young daughters, is the site administrator of LitPick Student Book Reviews and the editor of Family Friend Poems. She also blogs about motherhood at TyneaLewis.com and writes for *Devozine*, a devotional magazine for teenagers. She is a 2016 International Literacy Association 30 Under 30 honoree.

ARLENE LILA lives in Fountain Hills, Arizona. She enjoys writing to encourage Christians, to help them draw closer to the Lord. She only began writing in the last six years. She has written for *Country Woman, The Secret Place, Breakthrough Intercessor, Pentecostal Evangel,* and *Lutheran Digest.* She is a retired RN and a widow with four children and four grandchildren.

NO PICTURE
AVAILABLE

TERI LYN wrote for a small newspaper in Kodiak, Alaska, for two years and has several articles published in university publications. She earned a BA in English Literature when her grandchildren were entering grade school, and then she earned an MA in Journalism when the older grandchildren were graduating from high school.

ELISABETH NATTER is a freelance writer and full-time caregiver. Her writing credits include blogs and articles for several websites and literature study guides. She and her husband enjoy spending time with their five children, most of who still live at home and are known to spontaneously burst into song. She loves to tell stories that touch the heart and lighten the load. Story2Write.com.

DIANE NUNLEY is a retired nurse and writes from her home in the Cumberland Mountains. She has been published in professional journals, devotional books, and has self-published Christian women's fiction.

JILL PRINTZENHOFF lives in upstate New York with her husband and their two daughters. She teaches high school science at Twin Tiers Christian Academy. When she's not in the classroom, she spends as much time as possible on family adventures, biking rail trails, kayaking local waterways, fishing, and writing. Her writing has been featured in both online and print publications. Jillprintzenhoff.com

NANCY RUEGG is a former elementary teacher and mother to three grown children. She and her pastor-husband served six churches over four decades of ministry. They recently retired to Ohio, near their two sons. If their daughter and her family would also move from the Northwest to Ohio, life would be near perfect. NancyARuegg.com

VERONICA A. RYAN has a Masters in Theology from the Augustine Institute, and has given talks to young people on topics such as the Paschal Mystery, Scripture and Confirmation. She is a contributor to *Lectio: The Eucharist* as well as a frequent author of the Augustine Institute's alumni newsletter. She resides in Omaha, Nebraska with her husband and two small children. VeronicasViolets.com.

A.D. SHRUM, after receiving his Bachelor's in Mechanical Engineering at Virginia Tech, worked six years at General Electric before choosing to stay home with his two boys in Anderson, South Carolina. During this time he rediscovered his love of storytelling and is currently working on a major Christian science fiction novel. He receives valuable insight from his loving wife, Dr. Kara Shrum.

SHARON GARLOCK SPIEGEL loved writing even as a young girl. She is the author of *Generations, Fall of Grace*, and *Held Captive*, and a contributor to *The Benefit Package*. An Assembly of God minister and self-described "Missouri Yankee," she and Roger, her husband of nearly fifty years, live in western Missouri and have three children and fourteen grandchildren.

RJ THESMAN is the author of the popular Reverend G books that tell the story of a woman minister who is diagnosed with Alzheimer's. Thesman is also a Certified Communications Coach who helps other writers find their writing plans and birth their words. Follow Thesman at RJThesman.net and check out the Reverend G books in the Life at Cove Creek series at CrossRiverMedia.com.

TIFANY TREES, a North Carolina resident, is the mother of three daughters and works in the legal field. These experiences have broadened her understanding of the world and how God's kingdom works. Her writing was born from a passionate pursuit to translate this knowledge for others to increase their vision of God's presence all around us.

CHERYL WEBER is based in beautiful Lancaster County, Pennsylvania, but has served in various nations through short and long-term missions. She has had devotionals published in *The Secret Place*, and in Faithwriters devotional, *The Great Multitude*. A variety of her short stories and articles have also appeared in take-home Sunday school papers and local periodicals.

the *benefit package*

30 days of God's
goodness from Psalm 103

MORE GREAT BOOKS FROM CROSSRIVERMEDIA.COM

UNBEATEN
Lindsey Bell

Difficult times often leave Christians searching the Bible for answers to the most difficult questions — Does God hear me when I pray? Why isn't He doing anything? Author Lindsey Bell understands the struggle. She searched the Bible for answers to these tough questions. Her studies led her through the stories of biblical figures, big and small. She discovered that while life brings trials, faith brings victory. And when we rely on God for the strength to get us through, we can emerge *Unbeaten*.

CARRIED BY GRACE
Debra L. Butterfield

A family member... a friend... someone you know has sexually abused your child. Tumultuous emotions buffet you from all sides. You're feeling lost and confused. Where do you turn for help? Part memoir, part devotional, author Debra L. Butterfield offers comfort for your heartache, practical guidance for daily needs, a biblical path to healing, and encouragement and hope along the way. Let yourself be *Carried by Grace* as you journey toward restoration.

THE GRACE IMPACT
Nancy Kay Grace

The promise of grace pulses throughout Scripture. Chapter after chapter, the Bible shows a loving heavenly Father lavishing His grace on us through His son. In her book, *The Grace Impact*, author Nancy Kay Grace gives us a closer glimpse at God's character. His grace covers every detail of life, not just the good things, but the difficult, sad and complicated things. That knowledge can give us the ability to walk confidently through life knowing God is with us every step of the way.

If you enjoyed this book, will you
consider sharing it with others?

- Please mention the book on Facebook, Twitter, Pin-
  terest, or your blog.

- Recommend this book to your small group, book
  club, and workplace.

- Head over to Facebook.com/CrossRiverMedia,
  'Like' the page and post a comment as to what
  you enjoyed the most.

- Pick up a copy for someone you know who would
  be challenged or encouraged by this message.

- Write a review on Amazon.com, BN.com, or
  Goodreads.com.

- To learn about our latest releases subscribe to our
  newsletter at www.CrossRiverMedia.com.

Made in the USA
Middletown, DE
23 December 2016